Learning the Language *of* Depression

THE DEPRESSION PROJECT

Learning the Language *of* Depression

Overcoming Communication Barriers so People with Depression Are Safe and Understood

WILEY

Published by John Wiley & Sons, Inc., Hoboken, New Jersey.
Published simultaneously in Canada.

For general information on our other products and services or for technical support, please contact our Customer Care Department within the United States at (800) 762-2974, outside the United States at (317) 572-3993 or fax (317) 572-4002.

Wiley also publishes its books in a variety of electronic formats. Some content that appears in print may not be available in electronic formats. For more information about Wiley products, visit our web site at www.wiley.com.

Library of Congress Cataloging-in-Publication Data is Available:

ISBN 9781394317288 (Cloth)
ISBN 9781394317295 (ePub)
ISBN 9781394317301 (ePDF)

Cover Design: Wiley
Cover Image: © Ali/stock.adobe.com, © macondos/stock.adobe.com, © Tatyana/stock.adobe.com

SKY10099579_030725

Contents

Introduction

As we at The Depression Project hear every single day from members of our three million person plus social media community, a *"language barrier"* often exists between people with depression and those around them — in the sense that many words, everyday expressions and non-verbal forms of communication can take on a vastly different meaning than they otherwise would when they are coming from someone who has depression. And, as we also hear every single day from members of our community, this language barrier can result in people with depression experiencing the following:

- Feeling all alone due to no one understanding what they are actually going through
- Being continuously judged, put down, and criticized
- Having conflict with the people they care about most, which can cause irreparable damage to those relationships
- Not receiving the support they need, and therefore being forced to fight their depression all by themselves
- Feeling significantly more depressed as a result
- Being more at risk of attempting suicide

Whether you have depression yourself or are supporting someone who does, we are sure you will agree that this is the last thing that people living with this debilitating illness need. So, to overcome depression's "language barrier," we put together this book. What follows is a chapter-by-chapter breakdown of exactly what it will cover, as well as what you can expect to learn by reading it.

Part 1: Depression's "Verbal Language Barrier"

- **Chapter 1: What People with Depression Actually Mean When They Say *"I Have Depression."*** When they tell someone that they have depression, it has been many people's experience for this to be misinterpreted as *"I'm sad,"* which results in them not receiving the amount of support that their illness warrants, and in many cases, being dismissively told to *"just snap out of it," "just cheer up,"* or *"just think positively,"* for example. Consequently, in this chapter, we will explain the key differences between depression and sadness, as well as share a wide variety of quotes from members of The Depression Project's community that describe what people with depression are actually going through — in order to help them feel like they are not alone, and to help their loved ones understand depression better. Additionally, we will also explain how friends and family members can respond when someone tells them *"I have depression"* — in such a way that rather than making that person feel misunderstood, frustrated, and even more depressed (like the way people sometimes respond unfortunately does), they instead feel understood, validated, and supported.

- **Chapter 2: What People with Depression Actually Mean When They Say *"I'm Fine"* or *"I'm OK."*** When people with depression say they are *"fine"* or *"OK,"* then it is indeed possible that they actually are. However, unfortunately this is often not the case at all, which is why in this chapter, we will share a variety of quotes from members of The Depression Project's community that describe what people with depression are often really going through when they say *"I'm fine"* or *"I'm OK."* Additionally, this chapter also includes several suggestions to help people with depression feel more comfortable being open about how they truly feel so that they do not have to suffer in silence, as well as several suggestions to help supporters create a "safe space" in which their loved one with depression can feel more at ease talking about what they are going through.

- **Chapter 3: What People with Depression Actually Mean When They Say** *"Leave Me Alone."* When someone with depression asks to be left alone, there are numerous reasons why they might genuinely want to be by themselves. However, as we often hear from members of our community, sometimes people with depression might tell someone to leave them alone even when they actually want that person to stay with them. So, in this chapter, we will explain why this is, as well as what their friends and family members can do in this situation to help their loved one with depression get the support that, deep down, they might really want.

- **Chapter 4: What People with Depression Actually Mean When They Say** *"I'm Tired."* Tiredness is a very common symptom of depression, however, there are major, *major* differences between "normal tiredness" and what we at The Depression Project call "depression tiredness." So, in this chapter, we will share a variety of quotes from members of our community that describe what people with depression are actually experiencing when they say *"I'm tired"* in order to help those with depression feel like they are not alone, and to help their friends and family members understand "depression tiredness" better. Additionally, this chapter also includes several suggestions for how friends and family members of someone with depression can effectively support them when they are feeling "depression tired," and what – according to our community members – they should avoid saying so as not to upset them, make them feel bad about themselves, and/ or cause them to feel even more depressed.

- **Chapter 5: What People with Depression Actually Mean When They Say** *"I Can't … ."* When someone is in the depths of a depressive episode, it is common for there to be many instances in which they say *"I can't … ,"* for example, *"I can't do my chores today," "I can't have a shower,"* and/or *"I can't get out of bed this morning."* However, in many circumstances like these, *"I can't …"* is often interpreted by friends and family members of someone with depression as *"I won't … ,"* and when this happens, it can result in that person with depression being put down, criticized, and being labeled as *"lazy."* Consequently, to try to prevent this from happening and instead help people with depression receive the compassion and support that they deserve, in this chapter, we will explain the reasons why depression can significantly affect a person's ability to function; share a variety of quotes from members of our community about what people with depression are actually going through when they say *"I can't …";* and highlight why *"I can't …"* certainly does *not* mean *"I won't …".*

- **Chapter 6: What People with Depression Actually Mean When They Say *"I'm Busy."*** As we often hear from members of The Depression Project's community, telling their friends and family members *"I'm busy"* is a common excuse people with depression might turn to in order to socially withdraw and be by themselves. However, when people with depression say *"I'm busy"* and decline to meet with someone – particularly if they do so repeatedly – then it can cause that person to conclude that they are, for example, *"avoiding them," "a bad friend,"* and/or that they *"don't care about them anymore."* So, to resolve this misunderstanding and help prevent this relationship conflict moving forward, in this chapter, we will share a variety of quotes from our community members that describe what people with depression might actually be going through when they say *"I'm busy,"* as well as some helpful, supportive ways for the people around them to respond when they say this.

- **Chapter 7: What People with Depression Actually Mean When They Say *"I Want to Go Home."*** When they are out with others, it is common for those with depression to want to return home earlier than the people they are with would expect them to – which can then cause those people to conclude that they are *"rude," "selfish," "annoying,"* and/or *"boring,"* for example. So, in this chapter, we will share a variety of quotes from members of The Depression Project's community about the actual reasons why people with depression might want to return home early, as well as several different steps that can be taken to eliminate this source of conflict moving forward, and instead help people with depression get the support they need in these circumstances.

- **Chapter 8: What People with Depression Actually Mean When They Say** *"I Don't Care."* When people with depression say *"I don't care"* in response to, for example, being asked for their input on something, being asked to make a decision, having someone share something with them, or when they are in the middle of an argument or a difficult conversation, it is common for the person they are speaking with to feel upset, offended, hurt, and/or to interpret this as that person with depression not caring about *them*. And, because this can be extremely damaging to any relationship, in this chapter, we will share a variety of quotes from members of The Depression Project's community that explain what people with depression actually mean when they say *"I don't care"* – which, moving forward, can help their friends and family members who are told this to realize that they are still cared about. Additionally, we will also share some helpful, supportive ways for friends and family members to respond to their loved one with depression when they say *"I don't care."*
- **Chapter 9: What People with Depression Actually Mean When They Say** *"I'm Not Hungry."* Although on the surface, *"I'm not hungry"* might seem as if it can only have one possible meaning, when this is said by someone with depression, it can also take on several additional meanings that when not properly understood, can lead to frustrations, hurt feelings, arguments, and people with depression and their loved ones growing apart from each other. Consequently, in this chapter,

we will share a variety of quotes about what people with depression actually mean when they say *"I'm not hungry,"* as well as several suggestions to help prevent the misunderstandings and relationship conflict that can surround this phrase.

■ **Chapter 10: What People with Depression Actually Mean When They Say *"I'm Having a Good Day."*** A big misconception surrounding depression is that if someone struggles with this illness, then it means they are miserable 100% of the time. Consequently, if someone suffering from depression says they are having a *"good day,"* then it can cause their friends and family members to falsely conclude that either they were previously *"faking it,"* *"making it up,"* *"looking for attention,"* or just being *"overdramatic"* when they said that they struggled with depression; or that if they did struggle with depression, that they have now *"fully recovered"* (which means that if at any point in the future they claim to be feeling depressed again, then they must be *"faking it,"* *"making it up,"* *"looking for attention,"* or just being *"overdramatic"*). Consequently, to overcome these misunderstandings that can leave people with depression feeling frustrated, upset and even more depressed, we will clarify what it actually means when people with depression say *"I'm having a good day."*

Part II: Depression's "Verbal Language Barrier" in the Context of Suicide in Particular

■ **Chapter 11: The Language People with Depression Use That Can Mean They Are Suicidal.** Before someone attempts suicide, there are often *verbal warning signs* that indicate that they are feeling suicidal; however, tragically, it is common for friends and family members of people with depression to not pick up on them. Consequently, in this chapter, we will highlight the language that people with depression use that can mean they are thinking about suicide. Additionally, we will also explain what friends and family members can do when their loved one with depression is feeling suicidal – in order to ensure that first, they are safe, and second, that they receive the appropriate level of help and support they need moving forward.

Part III: Depression's "Nonverbal Language Barriers"

- **Chapter 12: Depression's "Facial Language Barrier."** When people with depression smile, avoid eye contact, have muted facial expressions, or look tired or frustrated, then it can mean something very, very different than it would if they did *not* have depression. And, because this "facial language barrier" can be yet another source of confusion, misunderstanding, and conflict between people with depression and everyone around them, in this chapter, we will clarify what people with depression are often actually going through when they smile, avoid eye contact, have muted facial expressions, or look tired or frustrated.

- **Chapter 13: Depression's "Touch Language Barrier."** There are multiple natural, understandable reasons why depression can cause someone to be much less tactile and physically intimate than they would otherwise be. However, if partners of people with depression are not aware of these reasons, then they are likely to take this physical withdrawal personally – which can lead to them feeling rejected, confused, angry, insecure in the relationship, and disconnected from their partner with depression. Of course, if they feel these emotions, then it will likely lead to conflict with their partner with depression and/or to them withdrawing themselves in response, which will likely then result in their partner with depression feeling alone, unsupported, and even more depressed, which will likely then result in their partner with depression withdrawing even more, and so the cycle continues and continues. Consequently, in this chapter, we will highlight a multitude of reasons why depression can cause people to shy away from physical touch and intimacy, as well as share the steps that both partners in the relationship can take to successfully navigate this "touch language barrier" moving forward, and prevent the cycle we just mentioned from severely damaging their relationship.

Conclusion

- **A Brief Recap + One Last Suggestion to Help You Continue Navigating Depression's "Language Barrier" Moving Forward.** At the end of this book, we will recap the most important points we have covered, as well as share one final piece of advice for how people with depression and those supporting them can continue breaking down depression's "language barrier" moving forward – which can help prevent misunderstandings and relationship conflict, result in that person with depression receiving the support they need from their loved ones, and contribute to them feeling significantly better as a result.

Are You Ready?

Now that you know exactly what this book will cover, we are ready to get started. Whether you are fighting depression yourself, want to better understand and support a loved one who is, or are just curious to learn more about this complicated illness that afflicts approximately 280 million people worldwide,[1] we really hope that you find it helpful – and are confident you will!

All our love,
The Depression Project Team

Depression's "Verbal Language Barrier"

1

What People with Depression Actually Mean When They Say *"I Have Depression"*

As we have heard countless times from members of The Depression Project's community, when someone with depression tells their friends or family members *"I have depression,"* it is very common for this to be interpreted as them *"just being sad."* However, depression is much, much, *much* more than *"sadness."*

First, unlike what is typical of sadness, depression is not something that afflicts someone for a brief period of time – such as for a few hours, a day, or a week, for example. Rather, as we hear every single day from our community members, depression can affect people for months, years, or even decades on end. And, for this reason, when someone says they are struggling with depression, it means they have struggled with their symptoms for far, *far* longer than just a few hours, a day, or a week.

Second, although prolonged, intense feelings of sadness and misery are indeed part of depression, this illness also encompasses a wide variety of other symptoms as well — some of the most common of which we will now identify.

Common Symptoms and Components of Depression (That Not Everybody Knows About)

- **Negative thoughts.**[1] For example, *"I'm a loser," "I'm unlovable," "I'm worthless," "I'm a failure," "I'm a burden," "I'm useless," "I deserve to suffer," "I'm not worthy of anything good happening to me," "everybody else is better and more important than I am," "I have no future," "there's no point in doing anything," "everything I do will be a failure," "I will never feel happy again," "I will never overcome depression," "none of my dreams will ever come true,"* and/or *"there's no point in being alive anymore."*

- **Feeling worthless.**[2] It can be common for people with depression to hate themselves, to struggle to see how any of their friends or family members could love them, and/or to wholeheartedly believe that everybody they know would be better off without them.

- **Feeling apathetic.** This includes no longer having interest in anything that they used to enjoy.[3]

- **Feeling numb.** In particular, it is common for people with depression to feel completely disconnected from the world around them, and completely disconnected from everything that used to bring them joy — to such an extent that rather than "living," it can feel as if they are merely "existing." This "numbness" can be caused by a variety of reasons, but most commonly, because people with depression might reach a point where they become desensitized to their own suffering, because numbness can be a defense mechanism to protect themselves from negative emotions,[4] and/or because numbness is often a side effect of antidepressant medication.[5]

- **Feeling completely and utterly exhausted.** This is another common symptom of depression,[6] often because, among other reasons, it is exhausting trying to function while being weighed down by depression's debilitating symptoms, and it is exhausting having to fake a smile and pretend that everything is "fine" (which can feel much more socially acceptable than saying *"I'm not OK"*). Additionally, difficulty sleeping and insomnia are also common symptoms of depression,[7] and feeling tired is a common side effect of antidepressant medication.[8]

- **Difficulty concentrating.**[9] This is often because, among other reasons, a person with depression's pain and suffering is consuming so much of their mental capacity that it reduces their ability to focus on anything else, because they are feeling numb and are disengaged from what is going on around them, and/or because their concentration is being interrupted by their intrusive negative thoughts.

- **Short-term memory difficulties.**[10] For example, according to members of our community, a person with depression might be unable to remember what someone was telling them in a recent conversation (which is why they might ask that person to repeat everything they said), they might be unable to remember that a friend sent them a message (which is why they might not respond to it), and they might be unable to remember that they have already purchased something they wanted to buy (which is why they might end up purchasing the same thing multiple times). In particular, these short-term memory difficulties are often a result of the fact that it can be extremely difficult for someone with depression to be able to focus, retain information, and be present in and feel connected to their day-to-day life when they are consumed with intrusive negative thoughts, painful emotions, feelings of numbness, exhaustion, and all the rest of depression's symptoms.

- **A significantly diminished ability to function.**[11] This is often due, as we have said, to feeling completely and utterly exhausted, having difficulty concentrating, and negative thoughts that can convince people with depression that they are not capable of doing anything. In particular, as we hear from members of our community every single day, depression can sabotage a person's ability to function to such an extent that even the simplest of tasks – including cleaning the dishes, having a shower, or getting out of bed, for example – can feel overwhelming and unmanageable.
- **Feeling irritable, frustrated, and/or angry.**[12] This is often due, among other reasons, to being constantly burdened by all of depression's symptoms, not being able to function anywhere near as well as they would like to, and/or having their depression be continuously misunderstood, minimized, and/or dismissed by the people around them.
- **Feeling extremely lonely.**[13] In particular, this is often due to the following reasons:
  - Feeling as if no one around them has any idea what they are going through (because, among other reasons, depression can be very difficult to put into words, and as we have said, faking a smile and pretending to be OK can feel much more socially acceptable than saying how they really feel).
  - Feeling as if no one understands the severity of what they are going through, how enormous a toll their depression can take on them, and how difficult this illness is to overcome (in particular, it is common for people with depression to feel especially lonely if their friends and family members make dismissive, frustrating, and/or hurtful comments such as, *"just snap out of it," "just think positively then you won't be depressed anymore,"* and/or in response to them struggling to function, *"you're so lazy"*).
  - Being physically by themselves due to socially withdrawing. In particular, people with depression might socially withdraw because, according to members of The Depression

Project's community, they have no motivation or energy to leave their home, because they feel too miserable to smile and pretend they are enjoying themselves, because they need time alone to process their emotions, because they need time to recharge their batteries, because they do not want any of their loved ones to see them at their worst, because they want to "protect" and to "shield" their loved ones from their pain, because they are worried that people will judge and think less of them for having depression, because they are worried that no one will understand their depression or take it seriously, and/or because they feel too ashamed of themselves to leave their home.

- **An existential crisis.** This can often take the form of ruminating on thoughts such as *"Why am I being put through so much pain?"* and/or *"Is this all there is to life?"*, which can contribute to people with depression feeling extremely lost and full of despair.

- **Engaging in destructive, self-sabotaging habits as a way of trying to cope with depression.** This often includes, for example, "comfort eating,"[14] alcohol abuse,[15] and/or self-harming.[16]

- **Shame.**[17] This is often due to the consequences that can stem from depression's intense, debilitating symptoms. In particular, according to members of The Depression Project's community, some of the most common consequences of depression that cause people to feel ashamed of themselves include an inability to function and get things done (including feeling so exhausted that they spend all day in bed), not being the person they want to be in their relationships, engaging in self-sabotaging behaviors that they later regret, decreased performance at school or at work, noticeable weight gain or weight loss, forgetting things that are special or important, and feeling so at the end of their tether that they are hypersensitive, which can lead to them breaking down and snapping over something trivial or lashing out at someone when they do not deserve it.

- **Physical symptoms.**[18] These can include, depending on the person, sleeping much more or much less that they otherwise would, significant weight gain or weight loss, feeling absolutely exhausted, body aches and pains, headaches, nausea, loss of appetite, and/or difficulty having sex (including impotency).

- **Feeling hopeless**[19] **and devoid of motivation.** When someone has been fighting depression for an extended period of time and despite their best efforts has not managed to get better, they might feel so beaten down and broken by their depression that they wholeheartedly believe that none of their dreams will ever come true, that they will never be happy again, and that they will be burdened with their depression for the rest of their days. And, if they feel convinced that this is the case, then it might be extremely difficult for them to see the point in doing anything – including, for example, setting goals and pursuing them, seeking help to get better, attending to their chores, looking after their personal hygiene, and even getting out of bed. Additionally, when someone with depression has lost all hope that their life will ever get better, it can cause them to feel suicidal[20] (and in the worst of cases, to act on these feelings).

Quotes from Members of Our Community About What Depression Is Like

The list of symptoms we just shared with you is not exhaustive, and as painful as they make depression sound, we still do not feel as if they do justice to just how consuming, devastating, and life-altering depression actually is. Consequently, we at The Depression Project asked members of our community to describe in their own words what depression is like, and next, we would like to share some of the responses with you:

- *"Living with depression is like having a parasite within you that drains your energy, and takes away any joy, hope, or meaning in your day-to-day life. It makes you feel numb, worthless, and empty, and often it's just easier to withdraw from people because it's difficult to explain to them what's going on, and exhausting to try to appear as if all is well. I feel as though I am stuck in a dark, deep, lonely hole that I'm desperately trying to find my way out of."*

- *"I don't know how to describe depression, except to say that it is so, so much more than just being sad. When you're temporarily sad, you might miss being happy, but when you've suffered from depression for as long as I have, you can't even remember what happiness is."*

- *"Depression is extreme, horrific, almost-unbearable mental pain that you can't see a way out of."*

- *"Depression is not just a 'phase' – it can go on for years and years, and you can't just 'snap out of it' no matter how desperate you are to. It feels like you're trapped in a dark hole like others have said, and no matter how much you try to search for the light, you can't seem to find it. It's completely exhausting, and sometimes, you are too numb inside to feel any emotion or to even know who you are."*

- *"Depression feels like you're slowly dying on the inside, but to the outside world, your illness is invisible. Someone has replaced your heart with lead and your blood with concrete, you've had the energy sucked out of you, and you've lost the ability to get excited about anything since even the slightest thing takes the biggest effort. You don't want to be alone, but you also don't want to have to make the effort to be in company. You're tired of being tired. Screaming on the inside. Trying to ask for help but either no sound is coming out or you're not being heard. People avoid you as much as you avoid them. It's extremely lonely."*

- *"This illness has consumed so much of me that I don't even recognize who I am anymore. I feel so disconnected from absolutely everything."*

- *"What is depression like? Even when I'm happy, I still feel as if there's something missing. I go through major slumps of numbness, because if I allow myself to feel that depth of despair, I don't know how I'd ever get up. Over-sleeping, under-sleeping, over-eating, under-eating ... clearly lacking consistency and stability. I always feel like an outcast."*

- *"You have no energy, and no matter how much you sleep, you still feel exhausted."*

- *"Depression is taking a shower sitting on the floor, because you don't have the energy to stand up and do it, but you know you still have to get ready for work. It's waiting until the last minute to get ready and get dressed before you leave. It's digging deep in order to function at work and then all but collapsing once you get home — sometimes bypassing eating because you just don't have the energy left for it. It's not responding to your friends' calls, texts, and messages because you don't have the social battery for it, and when you finally get around to doing so, you feel bad for taking so long. It's not showering for days because even the thought of it exhausts you. It's letting yourself go in ways you wouldn't normally do, and then feeling even worse about yourself as a result."*

- *"Depression impacts how my brain works. I have a hard time speaking, listening, remembering, thinking. This negatively impacts my self-esteem and confidence, making me feel like I can't 'handle life.' Without that confidence, it is hard to be hopeful about the future."*

- *"It's not being able to open emails and letters. It's needing a clean house to reduce your depression but having no energy to clean. It's always feeling flat and close to tears, but you don't know why. It's not being your best self for your family even though you want to be. It's disorganization and a general apathy to things that require your attention. It's sleeping too much or sleeping too little. It's a lack of self-care and not finding joy in the things you used to do."*

- *"I feel invisible while the world carries on around me … like I'm on a treadmill constantly walking but getting nowhere."*

- *"Depression is not wanting to open your eyes in the morning because you dread being awake and having to face your depression. It's not doing things you used to enjoy or love doing. It's not wanting to see people, and instead lying on the sofa or bed and watching endless movies or series because it's better than facing the outside world. It's not eating until it hurts your belly. It's seeing no light at all at the end of the tunnel, and having no hope for a better future."*

- *"Depression makes my life feel like a horror movie. Most of the time it's quiet, very dark, and tinged with dread."*

- *"There's no happiness in anything. The voices in my head are always negative, and tell me that the world would be a better place without me* in it. No matter how many people try to support me and cheer me up, none of their positivity sinks in. The darkness never fades."

- "Depression makes me loathe my life and everything about it."

- "It's so deeply painful thinking that because of your depression, you can't live the life you dreamed of as a child … or even just the life of an average person."

- "It feels like I've lost myself to depression. I used to be fun, outgoing, and sociable. I used to like trying new things, meeting new people, and going to parties, events, etc. But I've become too weighed down by depression to be that person, and I no longer know who I am anymore."

- "Depression makes me feel like my time on earth is a complete and utter waste. When you don't think you'll ever be happy again, it's easy to then start to think, 'What's the point in even being alive?'"

- "It's like you're adrift in the sea with no anchor, and no idea where to get one."

- "It's like the dementors from Harry Potter have sucked all the life out of you."

- "Having depression is like sitting on the bank of a river watching life continue over on the other side — but you can't cross to join in."

- "When it gets really bad, depression convinces you that there's never truly a light at the end of the tunnel. You think you see one, but it's just an illusion. You might feel a tiny glimmer of happiness … a fleeting moment of serenity … but then the darkness folds over you and you're engulfed once again. Then, once again, you start feeling as if you'll never be free of it."

- "I have all these goals and ambitions, but depression is like a weight holding me down, making it such a struggle to achieve even the littlest thing."

- "Having depression feels like drowning when you're surrounded by people … but none of them can reach you."

- "You're so consumed with depression that it's difficult to concentrate and remember things. I've forgotten friends' birthdays, what I ate for breakfast, things that I've bought, and things that I'm supposed to do."

- *"I can no longer work because my depression is so bad. And of course, the financial implications and needing help from other people make me feel even more depressed."*

- *"You get called 'lazy' by people who don't understand why you can't manage to clean your home or get out of the house. They don't understand how exhausted and hopeless depression can make you feel and how it kills your motivation. At least with a physical illness, most people will help and support you – but for depression, you get judged and criticized, which makes you feel even worse."*

- *"Depression is like a rain cloud hanging over you constantly. Even though it could be a sunny day, that cloud keeps raining on you."*

- *"When I wake in the morning, it can take me three hours to get out of bed to make a brew. I feel emotionally drained and the smallest of tasks seem like such a huge chore. I usually don't answer the phone or the door, and often don't bother to wash. I've gradually lost interest in everything. I've socially withdrawn. Each day, I long for the evening when I can sleep and be oblivious to my emotional pain again."*

- *"Depression is torture because on the one hand you hate feeling alone and are desperate for support, but on the other hand you're scared of being judged and of people thinking you're a burden."*

- *"When you have depression, everything becomes heavier. Every single thing."*

- *"Depression suffocates you to the point where you just stop caring about anything. What should I wear today? Don't care. It's my birthday today. Don't care. My city's team won the championship and everyone's celebrating. Don't care. I feel too numb to have any emotions."*

- *"I loathe the person depression has made me become – messy, disorganized, bad hygiene, alone, overweight from comfort eating, and being too exhausted to get out of bed."*

- *"Depression is self-hatred. It's self-harming as a result. It's wishing you were dead because you think everyone would be better off without you."*

- *"For me, depression means having this rage inside because I don't want to live anymore but I keep waking up."*

If You Have Depression Yourself

If you can relate to having your depression misinterpreted as sadness, then we hope that the symptoms of depression and the quotes we have just shared with you from members of The Depression Project's community have helped you feel more understood, and helped you see that you are not alone in what you are going through.

If You Do Not Have Depression but You Know Someone Who Does

Of course, rather than because you have depression yourself, you might be reading this book because you know someone who does and you would like to better understand what they are going through. If this is the case, then we hope the symptoms of depression we have shared with you along with the quotes about what depression is like help provide an insight into what people actually mean when they say *"I have depression,"* as well as make it clear that what they are going through is far, *far* more devastating, complicated, and life-affecting than being temporarily sad is.

Furthermore, because depression is much more devastating, complicated, and life-affecting than sadness, when someone tells you *"I have depression"*:

- It is very important that you do not respond to them in a way that implies that their depression is similar to sadness – because this is likely to make that person with depression feel misunderstood, frustrated, and even more depressed.
- Instead, we encourage you to respond in a way that is cognizant of the fact that their depression is something much more severe than sadness – which is likely to make them feel understood, validated, and supported.

On that note, we would now like to share with you a list of ways to respond to someone you care about with depression that are likely to make them feel misunderstood, frustrated, and even more depressed, as well as a second list of alternative ways to respond that will likely make them feel understood, validated and supported.

Example Ways to Respond to Someone Who Tells You "I Have Depression" That Are Likely to Make Them Feel Misunderstood, Frustrated, and Even More Depressed

- *"We all have bad days now and then."* Again, because depression is much more than feeling temporarily sad for a few days, rather than making your loved one with depression feel better, comments like this are much more likely to upset and alienate them.
- *"I know how you feel."* If you have personally experienced depression before, then this can be a nice, empathetic thing to say, because it can make your loved one feel less alone, and can help them feel more comfortable opening up and talking to you about their own battle with depression. However, if you have never experienced depression before, then although you no doubt know how being sad feels, you do *not* know how it feels to suffer from depression – and as a result, this comment is once again likely to make your loved one with depression feel misunderstood, frustrated, and even more depressed.
- *"Try to look on the bright side."* When someone is feeling sad, then perhaps *"looking on the bright side"* of whatever it is that is making them sad can cause them to feel better. However, depression is far, *far* too severe, multifaceted, and deep-seated to be able to be solved by simply *"looking on the bright side."* Consequently, this comment is also likely to rub your loved one with depression the wrong way.
- *"Cheer up, you'll be all right."* / *"Don't worry, it will pass."* Although sadness is temporary and passes sooner or later, depression can last for months, years, or even decades, and recovering from depression to the point of being free of its debilitating symptoms requires a *lot* of work. Consequently, comments like *"cheer up, you'll be all right"* and *"don't worry, it will pass"* are very flippant, dismissive comments to make about an illness as long-lasting, life-altering, and challenging to overcome as depression.

■ *"Just do [insert simple suggestion] – then you'll feel better."* As we often hear from members of our community, when they tell someone *"I have depression,"* it is common for them to be offered all kinds of simplistic, quick-fix advice – such as, for example, *"you just need to get out more," "just go for a walk," "go for a run to help you snap out of it," "do some meditation and then you'll feel better," "have a nice cup of tea and then you'll be alright," "just have a good night's sleep tonight and you'll feel back to normal tomorrow,"* or *"you can beat the blues by going to the gym and exercising more."* However, although this kind of simplistic, quick-fix advice might help someone stop feeling so sad – and although some of these suggestions might form part of a much broader, much more multifaceted treatment plan to overcome depression – depression is far, far, *far* too severe, complicated, and deep-seated of an illness to be quickly solved by any one of these suggestions alone. Consequently, simplistic, quick-fix suggestions such as these that minimize how debilitating and complex depression is – rather than helping your loved one with depression – are very likely to instead leave them feeling misunderstood, frustrated, and even more depressed.

■ *"You can't be depressed – you've got such a good life!"* Although this comment does not imply that depression is similar to – or the same as – sadness like the other comments we just mentioned, it is still one that is consistently brought up when we ask members of The Depression Project's community what the *worst* things to say to people with depression are. This is because although somebody might appear to have a good life on the *outside,* for any number of reasons that are not immediately obvious, it is still entirely possible for them to be struggling mightily on the *inside.* And, when this is the case for someone with depression, it can come across as very dismissive, hurtful, and upsetting when they are told that they *"can't be depressed"* because they have *"such a good life."*

Alternative Ways to Respond to Someone Telling You "I Have Depression" That Are Likely to Make Them Feel Understood, Validated, and Supported

Instead of the comments that we just shared with you, if someone tells you *"I have depression,"* then we encourage you to respond with something along the lines of the following:

- *"I'm so sorry to hear this. I understand that depression can affect different people in different ways, so to help me understand you better, would you feel comfortable telling me more about what you're going through?"* This response shows care, empathy, the understanding that depression can present itself in many different ways, and a willingness to listen and learn more about what your loved one is going through – all of which will contribute to them feeling understood, validated, and supported.

- *"Please know that I'm always here for you if you ever feel the urge to reach out."* This response acknowledges the severity of depression and shows your loved one that they are not alone in their battle with it. Once again, this will also help them feel understood, validated, and supported.

- *"Would you like to talk about what you're going through? I know talking about depression can be hard, but I'd like to hear more if you'd feel comfortable sharing."* This open-ended invitation gives your loved one the chance to talk about whatever aspects of their depression they feel the most willing or in need to open up about. This can not only help them to feel unburdened, but also, it gives you the opportunity to better understand what they are going through. And, the more you are able to understand them moving forward, the more effectively you will be able to support them

- *"I don't fully understand what you're going through, but I'm here to support you anyway."* Depression is a very complicated illness that can affect a person in many different ways, and can affect different people in different ways as well. Additionally, as we have touched on, it can also be very challenging to properly understand depression unless you have experienced it yourself. For these reasons in particular, it is understandable if you find it difficult to fully understand what your loved one is going through. However, the fact that you are trying your best to and are willing to support them is still something that they will no doubt appreciate and feel very grateful for.

- *"It's very brave of you to open up about your depression. How can I best help you moving forward?"* The first part of this comment shows that you are in tune with the fears that people often have when it comes to opening up about their depression, and the second part shows a clear intention to want to not only support your loved one with depression, but to do so in the ways that would be most beneficial to them. Consequently, this response is, once again, highly likely to be very much appreciated and very warmly received by your loved one with depression.

- *"I'm really glad you told me about your depression because I'd hate for you to suffer in silence, and I want to try to help you in any way I can."* It is very common for people to feel scared and hesitant to tell someone that they have depression – often because, to quote members of The Depression Project's community, they fear that they will *"bring them down"* and/or *"become a burden to them."* For this reason, telling your loved one with depression that you are glad they confided in you about what they are going through can really help to ease these concerns. Additionally, telling them that you want to be there to help them throughout their fight with depression will also contribute to them feeling extremely supported.

Next: What People with Depression Actually Mean When They Say *"I'm Fine"* or *"I'm OK"*

In this first chapter of this book, to overcome the "language barrier" that can exist between people with depression and those around them when they say *"I have depression"*:

- First, we explained in detail the differences between depression and sadness.
- Second, we identified how people around someone with depression can respond to being told *"I have depression"* in ways that rather than making that person feel misunderstood, frustrated, and even more depressed, instead makes them feel understood, validated, and supported.

Next, in Chapter 2, we are going to cover what people with depression actually mean when they say *"I'm fine"* or *"I'm OK."* So, as soon as you are ready, please turn the page so that we can begin.

2

What People with Depression Actually Mean When They Say *"I'm Fine"* or *"I'm OK"*

The second commonly misunderstood phrase that we would like to focus on in this book is *"I'm fine,"* *"I'm OK,"* or some variation thereof. Now, of course, when people with depression say *"I'm fine"* or *"I'm OK,"* it is indeed possible that they actually are *"fine"* or *"OK."* However, this sadly often is not the case at all. In particular, when we at The Depression Project asked members of our community, *"What do you really mean when you say 'I'm fine' or 'I'm OK'?"*, the responses included the following:

■ *"I say I'm fine because I don't want to be a burden to others, but on the inside, I'm dying."*

19

- *"I'm about to break, but I don't want to say it out loud."*
- *"I'm not fine, but I don't know how to describe all of my feelings properly."*
- *"When I say I'm fine, I really want people to notice that I'm NOT fine."*
- *"I don't have the courage to say that I'm broken."*
- *"I'm not OK at all. I just don't want to bother anyone with my depression."*
- *"I'm not fine – I'm just telling people what I think they want to hear."*
- *"When I say 'I'm fine,' what I'm really saying is 'I need help'."*
- *"Something's wrong, but I don't know how to talk about it."*
- *"I'm far from 'fine,' but I say 'I'm fine' because it feels like the only socially acceptable way of responding to the question 'how are you?'"*
- *"I'm drowning, but I don't know how to put this into words."*
- *"My depression hasn't become inconvenient enough yet to bother others with it."*
- *"I'm anything but fine, but what if I tell the truth and no one believes me?"*
- *"I'm too scared to ask for help."*
- *"I don't want to talk about how I'm really feeling."*
- *"I'm falling apart."*
- *"I really need help, but I don't want to trouble anyone."*

Steps That People with Depression and Their Supporters Can Take to Overcome the "Language Barrier" That the Phrase *"I'm Fine"* or *"I'm OK"* Can Give Rise To

As the quotes highlight, there are various reasons why someone with depression might hide how they really feel, and say *"I'm fine"* or *"I'm OK"* even when they are not. However, as understandable as this is, when someone with depression hides how they really feel – and when the people around them understandably believe that they are *"fine"* or *"OK"* as a result – it can sadly leave that person with depression

- Feeling misunderstood
- Feeling alone and isolated
- Not receiving any support from their loved ones
- Feeling even more depressed as a result

For these reasons, we think it is extremely important to *empower people to feel more comfortable being open about how they really feel when they are in a depressive episode*, instead of feeling as if they have to hide their depression by saying *"I'm fine"* or *"I'm OK."* And, with this objective in mind, here is a breakdown of what this chapter will cover:

- Because a big reason why it is so common for people to hide their depression by saying *"I'm fine"* or *"I'm OK"* is, to paraphrase our community members, they *"don't know how to describe their feelings"* or *"put their struggle into words,"* we will share with you the Storm to Sun Framework. As you will soon see, this can help people with depression quickly, easily, and accurately express how they are feeling in a way that can be immediately understood by their loved ones.
- Like several of the quotes we shared with you touched on, not wanting to be a *"burden"* to their loved ones is another common reason why people with depression might say *"I'm fine"* or *"I'm OK"* even when they are not. And, if you can relate, then to help you feel more comfortable being open about how you really feel, we will explain the thinking traps that people with depression often fall into that can falsely convince them they are a *"burden,"* as well as what we encourage you to remind yourself of moving forward to help you let go of the negative thought, *"I will become a burden if I say how I really feel when I'm in a depressive episode."*
- Last, we will talk about the steps that those supporting someone with depression can take to create a "safe, judgment-free space" for them to feel comfortable being open about how they really feel instead of hiding it.

The Storm to Sun Framework: A Potential Solution for People Who Struggle to Put Their Depression into Words, and for Their Supporters Who Want to Be Able to Instantly Understand How Their Loved One Is Feeling in Any Given Moment

As we have said, a common reason why people with depression might say *"I'm fine"* or *"I'm OK"* even when they are not "fine" or "OK" is because when they are in a depressive episode, it can feel impossible to accurately put everything they are going through into words. In particular, according to members of The Depression Project's community, this is because of the following reasons:

- *"Depression has so many different symptoms that can all be impacting you at any one time. I never know where to begin in trying to explain them all."*

- *"There is no vocabulary for depression. Yes, you feel miserable, sad, bad, tired, fed up, etc., but none of these words do any justice to just how crippling and soul-destroying depression actually is."*

- *"I think the main reason depression is so hard to explain is because it's invisible. If I had a broken leg, I could just point to it and say, 'see, this is what's wrong with me. This is why I'm struggling to do things.' But when you have depression, there's nothing to point to, and when you look perfectly fine on the OUTSIDE, it can be really hard to try to get across to someone just how terrible you feel on the INSIDE. There's just such a big disconnect there."*

- *"Sometimes depression makes you feel numb and causes you to emotionally shut down. When that happens, it can be hard to even talk let alone express yourself properly."*

- *"I can't concentrate when I'm in a depressive episode. Trying to put everything I'm feeling into words is beyond me."*

- *"I don't even understand my depression myself, so how can I possibly explain it to anybody else?"*

If you can relate to finding it difficult to express how you feel when you are in a depressive episode, then we would now like to introduce you to the Storm to Sun Framework. This was created by professional counselor and Depression Project cofounder Mathew Baker to achieve the following objectives, among others:

- Make it significantly easier for you to quickly put your depression into words.
- Make it significantly easier for the people around you to instantly understand how you are feeling in any given moment.

The Storm to Sun Framework

When you have depression, at any given time, you can be said to be in either the "Storm Zone," the "Rain Zone," or the "Cloud Zone" of the Storm to Sun Framework. And, before we show you how the Storm to Sun Framework can make it significantly easier for you to put your depression into words, we will first give you a detailed explanation of each of these zones.

The Storm Zone

- **Intensity of symptoms:** Severe
- **Ability to function:** Low

You can be said to be in the Storm Zone when the symptoms of your depression are severe – that is, when it feels like there is a storm raging in your mind. In this zone:

- You are usually being bombarded with negative thoughts, and those negative thoughts are at their most intrusive, most uncontrollable, most catastrophic, and you are most attached to those negative thoughts (i.e. more so than at any other time, you believe them to be true).
- Emotions like misery, shame, worthlessness, lack of motivation, overwhelm, numbness, irritability, and hopelessness, for example, are felt more intensely than ever.

- Your ability to function tends to be significantly compromised – to such an extent that fulfilling your day-to-day responsibilities can feel unmanageable (and often are), and what would otherwise be simple tasks like having a shower, brushing your teeth, taking the garbage out, cleaning the dishes, and/or getting out of bed for example can feel like climbing a mountain.

- Because the symptoms of your depression are at their most severe in the Storm Zone, you might feel the urge to socially withdraw and just be by yourself. Alternatively, if you do happen to interact with someone, then faking a smile and pretending to be "OK" might feel impossible, and you might accidently snap at them when they do not deserve it, you might find it very difficult to concentrate and stay engaged in the conversion, and at some point, you might shut down and become noncommunicative. After the conversation, you might also find that you have forgotten much (or even all) of what was said.

- It is common to engage in self-sabotaging behaviors (such as binge eating, substance abuse, and/or self-harm) as a way of dealing with depression's severely intense symptoms.

- Any physical symptoms of depression (such as exhaustion, difficulty sleeping, sexual dysfunction, loss of appetite, and/or body aches and pains) will be felt at their strongest.

- In the Storm Zone, it is common to feel so miserable, broken, and hopeless that you are unable to envision the storm ever passing.

The Rain Zone

- **Intensity of symptoms:** Moderate
- **Ability to function:** Moderate

You can think of yourself as being in the Rain Zone when the symptoms of your depression are moderately intense. In this zone:

- Metaphorically speaking, the storm in your mind has calmed down or not yet started – but it could flare up on short notice.

- While you still in all likelihood struggle with negative thoughts, they are less uncontrollable, less intrusive, less constant, less catastrophic, and you are less attached to them than when you are in the Storm Zone.

- Although you still have to deal with difficult, painful emotions such as worthlessness, overwhelm, irritability, and/or lack of motivation, for example, when you are in the Rain Zone, the severity of these emotions is considerably less intense than is the case in the Storm Zone.

- When you are in the Rain Zone, because the symptoms of your depression are less intense than they are in the Storm Zone, your ability to function is also higher, and as a result, relatively simple tasks like getting out of bed, having a shower, or cleaning the dishes, for example, will not feel akin to climbing a mountain like they might do when you are in the Storm Zone. In fact, when you are in the Rain Zone, you can usually uphold your day-to-day responsibilities – including doing the relatively simple tasks that we just mentioned, in addition to, for example, going to work and/or taking care of your children. However, although manageable, upholding responsibilities such as these while dealing with moderately severe symptoms of depression can affect you in various ways, for example:
  - It can make you feel tired and burned out much quicker than you otherwise would.
  - Because your ability to function is still compromised and you are consequently often at the end of your tether, then you might be prone to snapping over something small.
  - In the Rain Zone, completing the day's "essential tasks" like getting ready for work, working all day, and then making the trip home, for example, is likely to consume the majority of your energy, and as a result, you often might not have much capacity left over for what could be deemed "nonessential" activities such as your hobbies or socializing, for instance.

- If you do happen to interact with someone when you are in the Rain Zone, then you might still struggle to be as engaged as you would otherwise be. Not only that, but there might also be times when you have difficulty concentrating, and/or when you forget something they told you (although not to the same degree as when you are in the Storm Zone).

- Due to the symptoms of your depression being severely intense and your ability to function being at its lowest when you are in the Storm Zone, then as we have said, it is common to find it extremely difficult (and often impossible) to do the things that you would otherwise do. And, for this reason, when you are in the Rain Zone, you might find that you have an extended "to-do list" / backlog of tasks to attend to due to putting off doing them when you were in the Storm Zone and all of your energy was focused on "surviving."

- Although depression's physical symptoms (such as exhaustion, difficulty sleeping, sexual dysfunction, loss of appetite, and/or body aches and pains) are often experienced in the Rain Zone, they will not be present to the same extent as they are in the Storm Zone.

The Cloud Zone

- **Intensity of symptoms:** Mild
- **Ability to function:** High

You can think of yourself as being in the Cloud Zone when the symptoms of your depression are mild (or perhaps even absent), and you consequently feel relatively well – in the sense that you are only being minimally affected by depression (or perhaps not being affected at all). In particular, in this zone:

- You are able to think at your clearest, as well as at your most positively. This does not necessarily mean that you will not experience any negative thoughts while you are in the Cloud Zone (although you might not). However, if you do, they will be relatively passive, controllable, infrequent, and mild in nature, and as a result, they will cause very little disruption to your day-to-day life.

- All the emotions associated with depression, such as misery, overwhelm, worthlessness, and hopelessness, for example, are at their mildest when you are in the Cloud Zone – and in the best of cases, they might not even be present.
- Because your depressive symptoms are at their mildest, your ability to function is also at its highest. For this reason:
  - You will be able to function fairly well without becoming easily tired.
  - You will be much more likely to want to socialize with your friends and family.
  - In the Cloud Zone, your motivation is also likely to be at its highest, and for this reason, you will be most able to do anything that you might have been putting off doing while you were in the Rain or the Storm Zone (for example, socializing, like we just mentioned, but also your hobbies, chores, or anything left on your to-do list).
- In the Cloud Zone, any physical symptoms of your depression are mild or nonexistent.

How the Storm to Sun Framework Can Help You Quickly, Easily, and Accurately Communicate How You Are Feeling

Rather than saying *"I'm fine"* or *"I'm OK"* because you do not know how to put what you are actually going through into words, an effective alternative can be to instead *tell your supporters whether you are in the Storm Zone, the Rain Zone, or the Cloud Zone of the Storm to Sun Framework.*

With that being said, let's now see how this can work in practice.

Example 1: When You Say You Are in the Storm Zone   When you tell someone you are in the Storm Zone, then this instantly lets them know that at this moment in time, your depressive symptoms are severely intense. In particular, *depending on what the Storm Zone looks like for you,* it could instantly let them know, for example:

- Your head is currently full of negative thoughts.
- It is very difficult for you to be able to think clearly and maintain your focus on anything.

- The emotions you are prone to experiencing when you are in a depressive episode – such as misery, shame, and feelings of worthlessness – are at their strongest.
- You are feeling extremely tired, which is making what would otherwise be relatively simple tasks feel too overwhelming.
- Now more than ever, you can use some support.

Example 2: When You Say You Are in the Rain Zone   When you tell someone you are in the Rain Zone, then this instantly lets them know that at this moment in time, your depressive symptoms are moderately intense. In particular, *depending on what the Rain Zone looks like for you,* it could instantly let them know, for example:

- Although your negative thoughts are not as intense as they would be if you were in the Storm Zone, they are still present, and therefore still making it more difficult than it would otherwise be for you to be able to think clearly and concentrate.
- Although you are not feeling as miserable, ashamed, and worthless as you would if you were in the Storm Zone, you are still experiencing these emotions to a moderate degree.
- Although you currently have enough energy to complete most of your day-to-day tasks, given the moderately severe symptoms of depression you are dealing with, doing so is challenging for you, and might leave you feeling burned out and exhausted.
- Although you do not need as much support as you would if you were in the Storm Zone, because you are still dealing with quite a lot, you would still appreciate some support and any help that can be offered to make your life a little bit easier.

Example 3: When You Say You Are in the Cloud Zone   When you tell someone you are in the Cloud Zone, then this instantly lets them know that at this moment in time, the symptoms of your depression are mild or nonexistent. In particular, *depending on what the Cloud Zone looks like for you,* it could instantly let them know, for example:

- Your ability to think clearly and concentrate is at its highest.
- You are feeling at your most energetic.
- You are able to function and manage your day-to-day responsibilities fairly well.
- Because you are currently feeling relatively free of your depressive symptoms, now is the best time for you to socialize and spend time with your loved ones, as well as engage in any activities with them that you might not have felt up to participating in when you were in the Storm or the Rain Zone.
- Because your depressive symptoms are currently mild or nonexistent, you do not need any support for your depression right now.

Identifying What the Storm, Rain, and Cloud Zones Look Like for You

Now that you are aware of what the Storm Zone, the Rain Zone, and the Cloud Zone are and how this framework can help you communicate how you are feeling at any given moment in time, we encourage you to think about what each of these zones look like for you, specifically. To help you do this, the Appendix includes a questionnaire that, through a series of check boxes and fill-in-the-blank questions, holds your hand through identifying what you, specifically, tend to experience when you are in each zone. Once you have completed the questionnaire, we then encourage you to share it with the people who you want to understand your depression better so that they can know what you are going through in the Storm Zone, the Rain Zone, and the Cloud Zone. We think this is something you might really benefit from, because moving forward, it will mean that rather than you struggling to communicate how you are feeling and therefore hiding your depression by saying *"I'm fine"* or *"I'm OK"* as a result, all you will need to do is identify what zone you are in, at which point, the person you are talking to will instantly have a snapshot of how you are actually feeling, what your current capacity to function is, as well as how you would like to be supported at that moment in time.

Does Not Wanting to Be a *"Burden"* Cause You to Say *"I'm Fine"* or *"I'm OK"* Even When You Are Not?

In addition because it can be difficult for people to express how they feel when they are in a depressive episode, as we have mentioned, another common reason that can make people say *"I'm fine"* or *"I'm OK"* even when they are not is because they believe that if they say how they truly feel, they will become a *"burden"* to their loved ones. And, if you can relate, then to help you feel more comfortable being open about how you really feel when you are in a depressive episode, we would now like to do the following:

- First, explain the thinking traps that people with depression often fall into that can falsely convince them they are a *"burden"* (and/or that they *will become a "burden"* if they say how they really feel when they are in a depressive episode).

- Second, we will also share some encouraging reminders that, moving forward, can help you to let go of the negative thought that you are a *"burden"* and/or that opening up about your depression will make you a *"burden."*

The Cognitively Distorted Thinking Patterns That Can Falsely Convince People with Depression That They Are a "Burden" (and/or That They Will Become a "Burden" if They Say How They Really Feel When They Are in a Depressive Episode)

"Cognitive distortions" are distorted thinking patterns that are grounded in some form of bias, and that can result in you viewing yourself and/or the world much more critically, judgmentally, and/or negatively than you otherwise would.[1] When you think negative thoughts, there is a strong chance that you are thinking in a cognitively distorted way without even knowing it, and for this reason, it is extremely important that you identify and bring awareness to the ways in which you might be doing so.

Why?

Because if you can recognize that your negative thoughts are the product of *cognitive distortions* – as opposed to being *accurate perceptions of reality* – then it will suddenly become much easier for you to dismiss them and push them from your mind (or at the very least, your negative thoughts will likely lose some of their power over you).

On that note, we would now like to highlight three cognitive distortions in particular that fuel the negative thought *"I'm a burden"* / *"I will become a burden if I say how I really feel when I'm in a depressive episode."*

Cognitive Distortion 1: Filter Thinking

Filter thinking is when you focus on only one particular aspect of a situation and filter out all of the other aspects – such as when you only focus on the "bad" or the "negative" in a situation and filter out all of the "good" or the "positive." And, when it comes to the negative thought *"I am / I will become a burden,"* it is extremely common for people to focus on the impact (or the potential impact) of their depression on their relationships (which they perceive to be negative), and at the same time, filter out

- All of the positives they *have brought* to their relationships in the past.
- All of the positives they *likely still bring* to their relationships in the present.
- All of the positives they *will bring* to their relationships in the future.

If this is something you recognize yourself doing now that we have mentioned it – or something you do unconsciously without being aware of it – then to free yourself from the negative thought *"I am / I will become a burden,"* it is important that you *stop* thinking with such a negatively biased filter, and instead start looking at things through a much more balanced lens. And, to help you do this, we encourage you to thoughtfully consider your answers to the following collection of questions, each of which is designed to help you increase your awareness of all of the good you *have brought, do bring,* and *will bring* to your relationships:

- *Reflect back on the history of your relationships with the people to whom you think you are a "burden" and/or the people to whom you think "I will become a burden if I say how I really feel when I'm in a depressive episode":*
  - *What are some fun, enjoyable experiences you have shared together?* For example, a great night out on the town, a nice holiday together, your monthly coffee meet-ups, a hike you went on in the forest together, and so on.
  - *What are some occasions throughout the course of your relationship when you treated them kindly?* For example, by buying them a gift for their birthday, standing up for them when another person criticized them, giving them a lift when they needed to go somewhere, babysitting their children, and so on.
  - *What are some occasions when you made them smile?* For example, by complimenting how nice they look, telling them a joke, sending them a funny video on social media, buying them flowers to brighten up their day, and so on.
  - *Is there anything you taught them throughout the course of your relationship and/or that you introduced them to that has had a positive impact on their life? If so, what?* For example, explaining a difficult concept that they did not understand in one of your subjects at school, introducing them to squash which they now really enjoy playing, recommending a new TV series that they have become a big fan of, and so on.
  - *Is there any good advice you gave them throughout the course of your relationship that has had a positive impact on their life? If so, what?* For example, with regard to their career, their relationships, parenting, and so on.
  - *What are some occasions when you have been there to support them when they have gone through a difficult time of their own?* For example, when they were in the midst of a bad breakup, when they were struggling with an illness or injury, when someone they cared about passed away, and so on.

- *Are there any occasions when you forgave them after they made a mistake, did something wrong, or hurt you in some way? If so, what are they?*
    - NOTE: If you have behaved in a way because of your depression that you are not proud of (such as lashing out at them in a way they did not deserve when you were at "breaking point"), then bringing awareness to the times when you have forgiven them for something they have done can highlight the reality that throughout the course of a relationship, there will be times when each person might say or do something they later regret, and that this does not automatically make them a *"burden."*
- *Are there any other positive contributions you made to their life in the past? If so, what are they?*
- *Reflect on your relationships with the people to whom you think you are a "burden" and/or the people to whom you think "I will become a burden if I say how I really feel when I'm in a depressive episode." What are some positive ways in which you currently contribute to these relationships?*
    - NOTE: If you think *"I'm a burden"* in particular, then due to your depression, you likely do not feel as if you currently contribute as positively to your relationships as you would like to. However, it is still important to bring awareness to and to stop filtering out the positive ways in which you do currently contribute (which also might be more than you have been giving yourself credit for).
- *Reflect on your relationships with the people toward whom you think you are a "burden" and/or the people toward whom you think "I will become a burden if I say how I really feel when I'm in a depressive episode." What are some positive ways in which you would like to contribute to these relationships in the future?*
    - NOTE: These good intentions are again proof that you are a good person who brings many positives to your relationships.
- *What positive characteristics do you possess that make you a good friend / partner / parent, and so on?*

- NOTE: As we have mentioned, when you are fighting depression, it is common to struggle with negative thoughts, feelings of worthlessness, and other symptoms that right now might make it extremely difficult for you to recognize all (or any) of your positive characteristics. And, if this is the case, we have included the following list of examples to remind you. Of course, not all of these examples might apply to you; however, some of them almost certainly do, and each one that does highlights how good of a person you really are.

  - Would you be there for a loved one in need? If so, it means that you are *caring and supportive.*

  - Do you tell the truth? If so, it means that you are *honest and sincere.*

  - Are you nice to people? If so, it means that you are *kind.*

  - Does your heart go out to people who are going through something difficult? If so, it means that you are *compassionate, empathetic, and of course caring* once again.

  - Do you stand by the people you love as opposed to betray them? If so, it means that you are *loyal.*

  - Are you reserved about your accomplishments instead of constantly showing off about them? If so, it means that you are *modest, humble, and down-to-earth.*

  - Do you sometimes take a step out of your comfort zone to try to improve your or your family's life? If so, it means that you are *brave and courageous.*

  - Do you try not to judge, criticize, or think less of other people who are different from you? If so, it means that you are *accepting.*

  - Do you take care of your partner when they are feeling sick? If so, it once again means that you are *loving, caring, and supportive.*

  - Do you share what you have with others? If so, it means that you are *generous.*

■ Are you open to learning new things and hearing different points of view? If so, it means that you are *open-minded*.

■ Are you mindful of your children's needs, and do you try your best to help them get met? If so, it means that you are an *attentive parent*.

■ Do you try to work through any issues you are having with someone and resolve them together? If so, it means that you are *flexible and willing to compromise*.

■ *Now, reflect on your answers to these questions asking about the positive contributions you have made, are making, and will make to your relationships, as well as about the positive characteristics you possess. Then, imagine that all of these answers applied to someone else. In this case, what would you think of that person? And, as all of these answers actually apply to you, what does this tell you about yourself?*

★★★

As we really hope that reflecting on these questions has helped you to see, there is much more good that you bring to your relationships than you give yourself credit for. And, the more you are able to break out of "filter thinking" and recognize this, then

■ The weaker the negative thought *"I am / I will become a burden"* is going to sound in your mind.

■ The more comfortable you will find being open about how you actually feel when you are in a depressive episode, as opposed to hiding what you are going through by saying *"I'm fine"* or *"I'm OK."*

Cognitive Distortion 2: Double Standards   Having "double standards" involves maintaining a different set of rules for yourself than you have or would have for other people. And, as we at The Depression Project often observe, when someone with depression tells themselves *"I am / I will become a burden,"* they are indeed holding themself to an unfair double standard that they would *not* hold their loved ones to.

To see if this is something that you currently do, we encourage you to ask yourself:

> *"If a loved one was in my position, would I think that they are a 'burden' (and/or that they will become a 'burden' if they tell me how they really feel when they are in a depressive episode)?"*

If you are like many people with depression, then chances are that you would *not* think that your loved ones are or will become a *"burden"* in this case. On the contrary, you might instead think something along the lines of the following:

- *"It's normal for friends and family members to support each other when they're going through a difficult time."*
- *"I really wish they weren't going through something as difficult and painful to live with as depression, and I'd like to do everything I can to support them through it."*
- *"It's OK for people to not be OK, and if someone I love is ever going through a difficult time, then I'd want them to reach out to me for help instead of suffering in silence all by themselves."*
- *"Depression is the burden, not them. After all, it's not their choice to suffer from it."*

And, if this is the case, then it highlights that rather than your negative thought *"I am / I will become a burden"* being grounded in reality, it is a distorted thought that is grounded in you having a much harsher, much more self-critical, much less self-compassionate standard for yourself than you have for the people around you.

Cognitive Distortion 3: Mind Reading   Mind reading is when you jump to conclusions about what someone else is thinking – or will think – in a given situation. And, when it comes to the negative thought *"I am / I will become a burden,"* a common way in which it is fueled by mind reading is when people with depression make the assumption that their loved ones would rather be doing other things than supporting them when they are in a depressive episode. And then, as a result of making this assumption, they then hide their depression by saying *"I'm fine"* or *"I'm OK"* when they are actually not.

However, just because someone makes the *assumption* that they will be a *"burden"* to their loved ones if they are supporting them in a depressive episode instead of doing the *"other things they would rather be doing,"* it does *not* mean that this assumption is actually true. And, if you can relate to mind reading in this way, then to help you see that this assumption might in fact *not* be true, we encourage you to ask yourself:

> *"If someone I loved had depression, would I want to know about it so I could try to support them? Or, would I rather they suffer in silence by saying 'I'm fine' or 'I'm OK' even when they are not?"*

In the same way that you would most likely want to know so that you could lend a helping hand, could it not also be the case that your loved ones likely would, too?

Encouraging Reminders That, Moving Forward, Can Help You Let Go of the Negative Thought **"I'm a Burden" / "I Will Become a Burden if I Say How I Really Feel When I'm in a Depressive Episode"**

Now that we have shared with you three cognitively distorted thinking patterns that commonly fuel the negative thought *"I am / I will become a burden,"* it is our hope that you are starting to see that perhaps this negative thought is not quite as true as you had previously thought it was. And, to help you continue to gradually let go of this negative thought moving forward – and feel more comfortable being open about how you are feeling when you are in a depressive episode as a result – we would now like to share some sentiments with you that we encourage you to remind yourself of and repeat to yourself the next time you think this negative thought:

- *"There are many good things that I bring to my relationships, and when I think that I'm being a burden, I'm filtering out and ignoring all of these things."*
- *"Needing support from my loved ones does not make me a burden. It's normal for friends and family to be there for each other when they're going through a hard time."*
- *"I deserve to have the same kind, compassionate standards for myself that I have for my loved ones."*
- *"I deserve to receive the same love and support that I would give to my loved ones if it was them who had depression."*
- *"In the same way I wouldn't want my loved ones to suffer in silence if they had depression, my loved ones wouldn't want me to, either."*
- *"Throughout any long-term relationship, there will be times when one person is going through a difficult time and could benefit from some support, and there will be other times when the other person is going through their own challenges and could use support, too. Right now, I'm the one who needs support, and when my loved one needs support sometime in the future, I'll be there for them."*
- *"My depression is the burden, not me. I did not willingly choose to suffer from this."*
- *"Just because I have the negative thought 'I am / I will become a burden,' it does not mean that this negative thought is true."*
- *"This negative thought is grounded in cognitive distortions, not in reality."*

Of course, it is possible that one or more of these reminders might not resonate with you. However, we hope that at least one or more of them *do* resonate, and if this is the case, then we encourage you to repeat it to yourself anytime you catch yourself thinking the negative thought *"I am / I will become a burden,"* in order to help you

- Combat this negative thought.
- Feel more comfortable communicating how you really feel when you are in a depressive episode, instead of hiding your true feelings by saying *"I'm fine"* or *"I'm OK."*

How Supporters Can Create a "Safe Space" to Help Their Loved One with Depression Feel More Comfortable Being Open About What They Are Going Through (Instead of Hiding It by Saying *"I'm Fine"* or *"I'm OK")*

In this chapter, to help people with depression feel more comfortable communicating how they actually feel when they are in a depressive episode instead of hiding their struggle by saying *"I'm fine"* or *"I'm OK,"* we have dedicated a considerable amount of time to

- Making it easier for people with depression – with the help of the Storm to Sun Framework – to put what they are going through into words
- Helping people with depression to cope with and let go of the negative thought *"I'm a burden"* / *"I will become a burden if I say how I really feel when I'm in a depressive episode"*

However, although learning how to express their feelings and let go of negative thoughts surrounding being a *"burden"* can be important steps for people with depression to take in order to become more comfortable being open about how they are feeling in a depressive episode, an important step for *supporters* to take is to try to create a "safe, nonjudgmental space" for their loved one with depression to do this in. And, if you have a loved one with depression, then to achieve this objective, we hope you will find the following suggestions helpful:

- If a loved one with depression tells you *"I'm fine"* or *"I'm OK"* when you ask them *"how are you?"*, instead of automatically assuming that they must therefore be *"fine"* or *"OK,"* we encourage you to instead ask them a follow-up question, such as, *"Are you actually OK, or are you just saying that? I'm here to have a proper chat about how you feel if you'd like."* This shows that, first, you genuinely do want to know how your loved one with depression is feeling – as opposed to someone who asks *"how are you?"* just to be polite, for example. Second, it also gives your loved one with depression a second opportunity to open up to you more if they would like to, and to tell you how they are really feeling.

- In response to this follow-up question, if your loved one with depression repeats that they are *"fine"* or *"OK,"* we still encourage you to take a moment to share your willingness to listen to them moving forward if they ever want to talk about how they are feeling. In practice, you could do this by saying something like, *"Just so you know, if you ever don't feel fine and want to talk about what you're going through, then please feel free to let me know. I'll always be there to listen to you and try my best to help."* If your loved one with depression is not *"fine"* or *"OK"* in that moment, then saying this might help them feel comfortable enough to open up – and if they still prefer not to right then and there, then it might help them feel more comfortable doing so in the future whenever they are ready.

- To make them more likely to feel comfortable being open about what they are going through when they are in a depressive episode moving forward, we also encourage you to check in on them from time to time to see how they are feeling and if you can do anything to support them. This consistent interest in their mental well-being and offers to help them will, over time, show your loved one with depression that you really do care about them, and that you genuinely do want to be there for them if they need support. And, as a result, rather than telling you *"I'm fine"* or *"I'm OK"* even when they are not moving forward, they are more likely to tell you how they are actually feeling.

Be Mindful of Your Surroundings!

Furthermore, as a piece of general advice, we also encourage you to keep in mind that the environment they are in can often play a big role in determining how safe and comfortable someone with depression might feel opening up about it. For example, in a large group setting where everyone is laughing and having a good time, your loved one with depression will likely be more inclined to try to "blend in" and hide their depression by saying *"I'm fine"* or *"I'm*

OK" when asked how they are. However, in a much quieter, more private environment that is more conducive to serious conversations, they might be more likely to open up about how they are truly feeling. For this reason, the first and second pieces of advice that we just shared with you – about following up to ask if your loved one is *really* OK and emphasizing your willingness to be there for them moving forward – are most applicable when you are alone with your loved one with depression, and the opportunity exists to have an intimate conversation with them.

Next: What People with Depression Actually Mean When They Say *"Leave Me Alone"*

In this chapter, to overcome the "language barrier" that can exist between people with depression and those around them when they say *"I'm fine"* or *"I'm OK"*:

- We shared quotes from members of The Depression Project's community that highlight what people with depression actually often mean when they say *"I'm fine"* or *"I'm OK."*
- We talked about the Storm to Sun Framework, and explained how people with depression can use it to make it easier for them to put their depression into words.
- We explained why rather than being a fact that is grounded in reality, the negative thought *"I'm a burden"* / *"I will become a burden if I say how I really feel when I'm in a depressive episode"* is often a cognitively distorted thought that is actually false.
- We suggested some simple yet effective steps that supporters can take to cultivate a safe, comfortable environment that will help make their loved one feel more inclined to be open about what they are going through when they are in a depressive episode.

Next, in Chapter 3, we are going to cover what people with depression actually mean when they say *"leave me alone"* – which, as you will see, shares some similarities to them saying *"I'm fine"* or *"I'm OK"* even when they are not.

3

What People with Depression Actually Mean When They Say *"Leave Me Alone"*

The next phrase we would like to talk about that can create a "language barrier" between people with depression and those around them is *"leave me alone."* Now, of course, when someone with depression says this, they might in fact genuinely want to be by themselves. In particular, this might be because they want to have some space, for example, to do the following:

- Compose themselves
- Work through their feelings
- Rest and recharge their batteries

- Break down and cry in private
- Be alone with their thoughts

However, according to members of The Depression Project's community, often when people with depression say *"leave me alone,"* what they are *really* thinking is, *"I want you here with me, but I'm scared of draining you and becoming a burden."*

Can You Relate?

If you have depression yourself and can relate to saying *"leave me alone"* even when you actually want the person you are communicating with to stay with you, then to help you feel more comfortable expressing how you truly feel, we would like to reiterate some of the advice we shared with you in Chapter 2 when it came to coping with and letting go of the negative thought that you are a *"burden."* In particular, we encourage you to do the following:

- Carefully consider the ways in which this thought could be distorted by *filter thinking, double standards,* and/or *mind reading,* and therefore not an accurate reflection of reality.
- Reflect on the reminders that we shared with you, choose one that resonates with you, and then repeat it to yourself anytime you catch yourself thinking the negative thought that you are a *"burden."*

It will not happen overnight, but the more you are able to work on coping with and letting go of the negative thought that you are a *"burden,"* then moving forward, the easier you are likely going to find it to communicate your true feelings to the people around you – as opposed to saying *"leave me alone"* because you don't want to be a *"burden."*

Our Advice for What to Do if Someone You Know with Depression Tells You to Leave Them Alone

Alternatively, if you do not have depression yourself but someone you care about does, then if they tell you to leave them alone, we encourage you to confirm whether this is something that they actually want. For example, by sayings something along the lines of the following: *"If you want me to leave you alone, then of course I will give you your space. However, if you actually want me to stay with you but just don't want to ask, then I'm more than happy to do that, too. Even if you don't feel like talking, I could just sit here with you for a bit of added comfort if you'd like, or do anything else that you'd prefer me to do. I really just want to help and support you in any way I can, OK?"*

After responding to your loved one with depression in this way, they will most likely reply in one of three ways:

- *By reiterating that they would like you to please leave them alone.* If this is how they respond, then we encourage you to abide by their wishes, because, like we said, there are multiple reasons why someone with depression might indeed like to be by themselves for a while. In saying that, though, after giving your loved one with depression their space, we encourage you to reach out to them shortly afterwards to let them know that you are thinking of them, and to reiterate your willingness to be there for them anytime they would like you to be. In practice, you can do this by, for example, sending them a message such as, *"I just wanted to message to say that you are in my thoughts. Please always feel welcome to reach out if there is anything I can do for you."* This will contribute to them feeling cared for, supported and not alone; and even if they do not take you up on your offer, receiving your message will likely still make them feel a little bit better.
- *Your loved one with depression might ask you to stay with them.* And, if this is the case, then we encourage you to follow through with your offer of doing so, and to do your best to support and comfort them.
- *Your loved one with depression might respond by hinting that they would like you to stay with them, but implicitly suggesting that you leave –* such as by saying something along the lines of, for example, *"you don't have to stay just to be nice," "you probably have better*

things to do than stay with me," or *"I don't want to waste your time and trouble you."* And, if this is the case, we encourage you to reiterate your desire to stay with your loved one and support them.

Next: What People with Depression Actually Mean When They Say *"I'm Tired"*

In this chapter, we have talked about the following:

- What people with depression might actually mean when they say *"leave me alone"*
- The importance of people with depression continuing to work on confronting and overcoming any negative thoughts they have surrounding being a *"burden"*
- What supporters can do to try to make sure that their loved one with depression gets their true needs met when they say *"leave me alone"* – whether that is to actually be left alone, or to be comforted and supported

And, although this chapter shared a few similarities to Chapter 2, in Chapter 4, we are going to focus on something completely different: *what people with depression actually mean when they say "I'm tired."*

4

What People with Depression Actually Mean When They Say *"I'm Tired"*

When people with depression say they are *"tired,"* as was the case with *"I'm fine," "I'm OK,"* or *"leave me alone,"* it often has a very different meaning compared to when someone who does *not* have depression says they are *"tired."* Or, to put it another way, there is an enormous difference between "normal tiredness" and what we at The Depression Project call "depression tiredness," which is the specific kind of tiredness that often consumes people with depression. Consequently, in this chapter

- We will share a variety of quotes from members of The Depression Project's community that explain what people with depression actually mean when they say *"I'm tired."*

- Building on these explanations, we will share some additional quotes from members of The Depression Project's community about the ways in which "depression tiredness" can affect people physically, mentally, emotionally, and behaviorally.

- We will share several suggestions for how friends and family members can respond when a loved one with depression tells them *"I'm tired"* – in such a way that rather than causing them to feel misunderstood and frustrated (which is how they will likely feel if their "depression tiredness" is equated with "normal tiredness"), they are instead likely to feel understood, validated, and supported.

- Last, we will talk about how adding context to the phrase *"I'm tired"* might be able to help people with depression be better understood by their friends and family members.

With that being said, as soon as you are ready, let's get started.

What People with Depression Actually Mean When They Say *"I'm Tired"* – According to Members of The Depression Project's Community

- *"I'm mentally, emotionally, and physically exhausted."*
- *"I'm tired of literally everything. Tired of negative thoughts, painful emotions, and people not taking my depression seriously. Tired of continually trying to keep on living when I feel like dying. Tired of always been tired. There is no end in sight."*
- *"I'm tired of being burdened with the weight of depression each day."*
- *"I'm tired of this joyless existence that depression has condemned me to. There is nothing to look forward to in my days … I just wait for them to pass until it's all over. I'm tired of not living, but just existing."*
- *"I'm tired of always having to pretend to be OK when I'm not."*
- *"I have no energy or motivation left to fight this illness."*
- *"When I say 'I'm tired,' it means I'm so consumed with exhaustion that I can barely do anything except lie in bed all day. Going to the*

bathroom feels like running a marathon. I can't shower, can't clean, can't even think about cooking — just eat cereal or toast. It takes all my energy just to survive."

■ "I'm tired means I've had enough of everything. I'm desperate for a break. Even the smallest task feels too overwhelming."

■ "My antidepressant medication is making me feel so heavy and slow and zonked out that I'm like a zombie."

■ "I'm tired from having yet another bad night's sleep because of my depression. When all the negative thoughts are bombarding my brain, I can't relax enough to sleep. After a while, I then get stressed because I know it's getting later and later and that I'm going to feel exhausted the next day — and this, of course, makes it even harder to relax and fall asleep. Sometimes this can go on for hours and hours, and then the next day, I'm a total wreck."

■ "Since some traumatic past experiences are major causes of my depression, I sometimes have nightmares that jolt me awake in a screaming panic. It usually takes me a long time to feel calm again afterwards, and then the next day, I'm always exhausted."

■ "I'm tired of having to be 'on' for others. Of trying to appear 'normal' and that everything is fine. I just want to stop pretending and collapse in a heap."

■ "I'm tired means I'm completely drained of emotions and energy. I'm numb. I can't get out of bed. I can't do anything. I'm not being lazy — I just have nothing left to give."

■ "My responsibilities are too much for me right now. I need a break. I need help. I can't go on."

■ "My tank is empty. I'm barely making it through the day."

■ "I'm tired of feeling tired no matter how much sleep I get."

■ "Everything is drained out of me: energy, optimism, motivation, hope for the future. I am just existing under a burden of awfulness."

■ "When I say 'I'm tired,' it means I'm in 'survival mode.' Please don't expect me to be able to do anything beyond just staying alive."

■ "I don't have the energy to keep on going. When will it end? I can't keep living like this."

■ "I'm tired of fighting every single day and never getting better."

How "Depression Tiredness" Can Affect People Physically, Mentally, Emotionally, and Behaviorally

As the quotes that we have shared with you show, the specific form of tiredness that so many people with depression experience is very, *very* different to "normal tiredness," and it can take an absolutely enormous toll on a person. And, to further clarify just how life-altering "depression tiredness" can be, we would now like to share with you some additional quotes about how "depression tiredness" can affect people physically, mentally, emotionally, and behaviorally.

Quotes About How "Depression Tiredness" Can Affect People Physically

- *"Your body feels so heavy that you can barely sit up when the alarm goes off. Then, after you've finally gotten up and gotten dressed, you feel so fatigued that you have to lie back down again."*
- *"The exhaustion is so consuming that it takes all your energy just to get out of bed."*
- *"It's that feeling of wanting to slump on the couch after a long day of work, except that it's there nonstop. Even when you do nothing but lie in bed all day."*
- *"It's like your body is lifeless ... or at least the 'aliveness' in it is much less than it would otherwise be. When I'm 'depression tired,' my legs feel heavy. I walk very slowly, and each step feels like an uphill climb. It feels like I could just lie down motionless forever."*

Quotes About How "Depression Tiredness" Can Affect People Behaviorally

- *"I become barely able to function. Even the little things like getting dressed, brushing my teeth, having a shower, taking the trash out, and doing the dishes can feel too overwhelming."*
- *"When the exhaustion overtakes me, I not only can't leave home to meet people, but I don't even have the energy to respond to messages on my phone. Sometimes, I go days without talking to anyone."*
- *"I become too tired to do the things that I know are good for me: no cooking healthy food, no exercising, no reaching out to meet people,*

etcetera. Instead, I stay in bed all day, watch old tv shows, and eat junk food. Then of course, I feel even worse about myself."

- *"Everything just takes so much more effort than usual. When I'm feeling exhausted in a depressive episode, even the things I usually love doing like walking my dog and playing the piano feel like chores that are beyond my capacity."*

Quotes About How "Depression Tiredness" Can Affect People Mentally

- *"I become too exhausted to be able to think clearly. My mind feels too hazy to be able to concentrate. On the occasions when I've tried to read a book, I end up rereading the same page multiple times but still not taking anything in."*

- *"There are times when I have trouble following a simple story that my husband is telling me. My mind just isn't alert enough to be able to keep up."*

- *"It's like my brain is unable to connect things together. I work in strategy, and when depression is making me exhausted, I really struggle to see a clear direction and create a game plan like I normally would. Then the self-abuse starts — my mind telling me things like 'you're letting everybody down,' 'you don't deserve to have the job you have,' ' you're going to get fired soon and be replaced with someone who's ten times better than you' — which, of course, just makes trying to think even harder."*

- *"When I spend the day in bed and accomplish nothing, I become even more self-critical than usual. Same when I can't push myself enough to do my chores."*

- *"It makes me forgetful. Sometimes I can't remember if I've taken my meds or not."*

Quotes About How "Depression Tiredness" Can Affect People Emotionally

- *"The thought of doing even the simplest of tasks causes me to feel overwhelmed, and my exhaustion is so consuming that it overpowers my motivation to do them."*

- *"It gets to the point where I feel empty. Numb. Disconnected from my surroundings. I know that I am alive but I am no longer living."*
- *"It makes me feel ashamed of myself. Ashamed of not showering, ashamed of not taking out the trash and letting the dishes pile up, ashamed of my room being a mess, ashamed of struggling so much to live and function like a normal adult."*
- *"When I'm so tired that I let myself go, then I really feel worthless."*
- *"I feel guilty for being unproductive and not living up to my potential."*
- *"It's just sad. I can't do the things I want to do, and I feel like I'm constantly falling behind despite doing my best with the energy I have."*
- *"I feel like giving up, because I'm too burned out to continue fighting."*

How We Recommend You Respond (and Do Not Respond) if Someone You Know with Depression Tells You *"I'm Tired"*

If you are reading this book because you know someone with depression and would like to understand them and what they are going through better, we hope the quotes about "depression tiredness" we just shared have helped provide an insight into the following:

- What people with depression actually mean when they say *"I'm tired,"* and how different what they are going through is to "normal tiredness"
- How debilitating "depression tiredness" can be, and the enormous physical, behavioral, mental, and emotional impact it can have on a person

And, because "depression tiredness" is very different from "normal tiredness" and can have such a life-altering impact on people like so, if a loved one with depression tells you *"I'm tired,"* then we'd like to share the following advice with you:

- Do *not* respond in a way that equates their "depression tiredness" with "normal tiredness," or that minimizes the severity of their "depression tiredness." After all, this is likely to make them feel misunderstood, frustrated, and even more depressed.

■ Instead, try your best to respond in a way that is sensitive to the fact that "depression tiredness" can be extremely debilitating – which is likely to make your loved one with depression feel understood, validated, and supported.

On that note, next, you will find a list of example ways to respond to your loved one with depression that are likely to make them feel misunderstood, frustrated, and even more depressed, as well as a second list of ways to respond that are likely to make them feel understood, validated, and supported.

Example Ways to Respond to Someone with Depression Telling You "I'm Tired" That Are Likely to Make Them Feel Misunderstood, Frustrated, and Even More Depressed

■ *"Just have a nap / a good night's sleep and then you'll feel back to normal."* Although this suggestion can fix tiredness that is caused by lack of sleep, it will not fix someone's "depression tiredness" – which as we have indicated, can be caused by, for example, how tiring it can be to be burdened by depression's symptoms every day, how tiring it can be to constantly have to pretend you are fine, how tired antidepressant medication can make you feel, how tiring it can be to have night after night of horribly disrupted sleep due to uncontrollable negative thoughts and/or nightmares, and how tiring it can be to continuously fight and fight to get better, but never feel as if you are making any progress. Consequently, rather than being appreciated by your loved one with depression, comments like *"just take a nap"* or *"have a good night's sleep tonight"* are much more likely to upset and trigger them.

■ *"What do you mean you're tired? You've been sleeping all day and haven't even done anything!"* Comments like this that invalidate your loved one's "depression tiredness" are almost certainly going to make them feel extremely misunderstood, frustrated, and even more depressed. Additionally, pointing out to them how little they have done throughout the day is also liable to make them feel ashamed of themselves, and intensify the self-critical voice in their head that, chances are, might already be tormenting them.

■ *"Just pull yourself together and do [insert task]."* This comment and others like it minimize just how severely "depression tiredness" can affect people, and as a result, they are also likely to make your loved one with depression feel very misunderstood, frustrated, and even more depressed.

Alternative Ways to Respond to Someone with Depression Telling You "I'm Tired" That Are Likely to Make Them Feel Understood, Validated, and Supported

Rather than making the previous comments, if someone with depression tells you *"I'm tired,"* we instead encourage you to respond with something along the lines of the following:

■ *"Given everything you're going through, it makes perfect sense that you'd be feeling exhausted."* This validates your loved one's "depression tiredness," and as a result will make them feel understood and less alone in their struggle.

■ *"Instead of [activity they said they were too tired to do with you], is there something that requires less energy that you would feel up to doing with me? Or, would you prefer to just rest?"* By not trying to pressure your loved one into doing something that they feel too tired to do and instead attempting to adapt to their current energy levels, you are showing respect for them and what they are going through.

■ *"Are there any tasks I can help you with or any chores I can do for you that could help lighten your load a little?"* When your loved one is feeling "depression tired," this is often a particularly helpful way of supporting them, because, like we have said, "depression tiredness" tends to make *absolutely everything* a struggle — including the "little things" like doing the grocery shopping, preparing dinner, washing the dishes, taking the trash out, and cleaning up around the house, for example. Consequently, any help you can give your loved one with depression – such as by helping them complete these everyday tasks, or by doing something else that they specifically ask for – is something they will likely be very grateful for.

- *"Any little task you complete when you're feeling depressed and exhausted is a win against this illness. You're doing much better than you think you are."* This response acknowledges how difficult it can be for someone to function when they are "depression tired," and by pointing out that your loved one with depression is actually doing a good job under the circumstances, it can help soothe any feelings of shame they might have as a result of not getting as much done as they would like to.

Each of these comments come from a warm, kind-hearted place, and are sensitive to the fact that feeling "depression tired" can be extremely debilitating. Consequently, rather than making your loved one with depression feel misunderstood, frustrated, and even more depressed, they are likely to make them feel understood, validated, and supported instead.

Our Advice for You if You Have Depression Yourself and Can Relate to Feeling "Depression Tired"

Alternatively, if you are reading this book because you have depression yourself and can relate to feeling "depression tired," then we hope you can take some solace in the fact that – as evidenced by all the quotes we have shared with you – you are not alone, and that what you are experiencing is completely understandable given everything you are going through.

Additionally, to be better understood, and therefore better supported, by your friends and family members instead of having them equate your "depression tiredness" with "normal tiredness," rather than making a general comment like *"I'm tired,"* you might find it helpful to try your best to reframe this comment in a way that is more detailed and specific to what you are actually going through. For example:

- *"I'm really tired from pretending that I'm fine all day, when on the inside, I feel miserable. So tonight, instead of going to the party, I'd just like to stay at home and watch TV to relax."*
- *"I feel so weighed down by all of depression's symptoms that I don't have the energy to do anything except the bare minimum to survive. Could you please help me out by doing [insert task that you find overwhelming]? I really would appreciate it."*
- *"I'm tired of constantly feeling depressed. Every day is full of misery and there is nothing to look forward to. I'm in a really bad place right now, and I can't see the light at the end of the tunnel."*
- *"I have no energy to do anything today, I'm sorry. I feel so exhausted from trying my hardest to overcome depression but still being burdened by it. I need some time to rest and recharge and to figure out what to do next."*
- *"My antidepressant medication is making me feel too tired to leave the house. What if instead of going out for dinner, you came over and we ordered something instead?"*

Given that the generalized phrase *"I'm tired"* is – at least by people who do not have depression themselves – most commonly associated with "normal tiredness," if you try to reframe this phrase in a more detailed, specific way that reflects the "depression tiredness" you are experiencing, it might help you to be better understood by the person you are talking to. Of course, this suggestion is not guaranteed to work – because "depression tiredness" can be difficult to put into words, and difficult for people who have never experienced it before to understand it properly. However, we believe it is still worth a try, and even if it does not help *everyone* you know understand your "depression tiredness" better, it will hopefully help at least *some* of the people around you to understand it better.

Next: What People with Depression Actually Mean When They Say *"I Can't ..."*

To overcome the "language barrier" that can exist between people with depression and those around them when they say *"I'm tired,"* in this chapter

- We highlighted what people with depression actually mean when they say *"I'm tired,"* as well as the many different ways that "depression tiredness" can affect them.
- We identified how those surrounding someone with depression can respond to being told *"I'm tired"* in a way that rather than making that person feel misunderstood, frustrated, and even more depressed, instead makes them feel understood, validated, and supported.
- We talked about how reframing the generalized phrase *"I'm tired"* in a more detailed, specific way that reflects the "depression tiredness" that a person with depression is experiencing might – at least in some cases – make it easier for them to be understood and supported by the person they are talking to.

Next, in Chapter 5, we are going to focus on yet another phrase that, as we continuously hear from members of The Depression Project's community, is often misunderstood by the people around them: *"I can't ..."*

5

What People with Depression Actually Mean When They Say *"I Can't ..."*

The next phrase we would like to talk about that can create a "language barrier" between people with depression and those around them is *"I can't ... ."* For example:

- *"I can't get out of bed."*
- *"I can't have a shower."*
- *"I can't do my chores today."*
- *"I can't go to work today."*
- *"I can't do [insert any other task]."*

Unfortunately, as we at The Depression Project have heard countless times from members of our community, when someone with depression says *"I can't ..."* – particularly when they are referring to something that the majority of people who do not have depression would find relatively easy to do – then it is often interpreted by the person they are speaking to as *"I won't … ."* And, when this happens, it commonly results in that person with depression experiencing the following:

- Being put down, criticized, and/or being called *"lazy"* for not doing that particular task.
- Consequently, feeling even more depressed.

However, it is extremely, *extremely* important to note that

- People with depression are *not* lazy!
- As we have previously mentioned, depression can significantly compromise a person's ability to function to the point where what would otherwise be relatively simple, easy tasks can become overwhelming and beyond the capacity of a person with depression. For this reason, when it comes to doing even simple tasks, a person with depression might justifiably say *"I can't."*

To emphasize this point in more detail, we will now

- Explain the reasons *why* depression can make it so difficult for people to function, and make them feel as if they cannot do relatively simple tasks that they would otherwise be able to do.
- Share with you a variety of quotes from members of The Depression Project's community that identify what specific tasks depression often make extremely challenging to do.
- Explain what it actually means when people with depression say *"I can't … ."*

The Reasons Why Depression Can Make It So Difficult for People to Function, and Consequently Convince Them They *"Can't"*

As we've talked about in detail in Chapter 4, it is very common for people with depression to feel completely, utterly, and debilitatingly exhausted, and when this is the case, it will significantly compromise their ability to function. However, although "depression tiredness" is arguably the biggest reason why depression can severely limit a person's ability to function, it is not the *only* reason.

In Addition to Making People Feel Exhausted, Depression Can Also Make It Extremely Difficult to Concentrate

As we mentioned in Chapter 1, depression can significantly compromise a person's ability to concentrate. In particular, to highlight the extent to which depression can affect a person's ability to concentrate, we asked members of The Depression Project's community:

"What does lack of concentration look like when you have depression?"

And, we would now like to share with you some of the responses:

- *"It's a blurry, empty space in your mind. It's always like a foggy day."*
- *"Needing to read the same thing over and over, because it feels like it's written in a foreign language and just not making sense."*
- *"I cannot get started on tasks. Cannot maintain any focus. It's a fog that others who have not had depression will never understand. It's like slogging through knee-deep mud."*
- *"Not being able to finish the tasks that you start. Sitting staring into space and then remembering what you 'should' be doing. Not being able to focus on anything anyone is saying, even if you're trying really, really hard to. Suddenly having to stop what you're doing so you can remember what you're doing. Making a list of chores so you don't forget what you have to do, but then forgetting what should be on it once you start writing."*
- *"Blankly staring at someone or something, then suddenly realizing you're out of it and then you go 'huh?' Zoning out during a conversation. Even though something was explained to you many times, you still don't get it. There is a very slow intake of information. You forget what is told to you. You keep asking questions about something even though it was addressed just a moment ago."*

- *"I start to think about doing something important or unimportant and within seconds, I have no idea what my plan had been."*
- *"Sometimes it dawns on me that I haven't got a clue what has been going on around me, because my mind has gotten lost in its maze of negative thoughts."*

As these quotes highlight, depression can significantly inhibit a person's ability to concentrate. And, when this is the case, it is very common for people to feel as if they *"can't"* do anything that requires even a very limited amount of concentration.

In Addition to Making People Feel Exhausted and Unable to Concentrate, Struggling with Depression Can Also Involve Battling Negative Thoughts That Can Convince People They "Can't"

As we mentioned in Chapter 1, it is extremely common for people with depression to think negative thoughts. For example:

- *"I'm a failure."*
- *"I'm weak."*
- *"I'm useless."*
- *"I'm hopeless."*
- *"I'm pathetic."*
- *"I can't do anything right."*

And, when someone with depression is consumed with negative thoughts such as these, it can cripple their self-worth and confidence, and convince them that they *"can't"* do things that they otherwise would be able to do. Furthermore, when that person with depression does not then do those things, their negative thoughts like *"I'm a failure," "I'm weak," "I'm useless," "I'm hopeless," "I'm pathetic,"* and *"I can't do anything right,"* for example, are likely to become even stronger, which will make that person with depression even more convinced that they *"can't,"* which will make them even less likely to do those things, which will make their negative thoughts even stronger, and so the vicious cycle continues and continues – often to the point where that person with depression no longer feels capable of anything.

Additionally, not only is it very common for people with depression to have low self-worth and confidence, but it is also common for them to *overestimate* how difficult the tasks they think they cannot do actually are. In particular, as one member of The Depression Project's community once put it:

> *"The more depressed I'm feeling, the more I'm likely to catastrophize things, and this includes thinking that things are more overwhelming and unmanageable than they actually are."*

Of course, when this is the case, it can also explain why someone with depression might believe that they *"can't"* do something.

Quotes About What Simple Tasks Can Be Overwhelming in a Depressive Episode

Now that we have identified the reasons why depression can drastically limit a person's ability to function, we would like to share – in their own words – the specific tasks that members of our community find overwhelming when they are in a depressive episode:

- *"When you're feeling depressed, everything in daily life feels overwhelming. And I mean literally EVERYTHING."*
- *"The simplest of things feel like climbing a mountain ... brushing my teeth, showering, changing my clothes, cooking food ... you name it, it's overwhelmingly exhausting."*
- *"It's overwhelming to talk to people. I just want to stay in bed all day."*
- *"When I'm feeling deeply depressed, washing my hair and applying face products is beyond my capacity."*
- *"Going to my kids' school activities and sports, family functions, going to the store ... it takes absolutely everything out of me."*
- *"Cleaning is unmanageable ... in particular the bathroom/toilet. At the moment, my room also looks like a bomb has gone off."*

- *"For me, some of the daunting tasks that feel overwhelming during a depressive episode are my college work and all the 'basics.' Even getting out of bed can be hard because I lack the energy."*
- *"I find it overwhelming to go outside and get the mail. If my letterbox is starting to overflow, then it's a sign my depression is getting bad again."*
- *"When you're feeling really depressed, cleaning your house is more overwhelming than anyone could possibly imagine. Friends and family think you're lazy and messy, but really, it is so exhausting to do anything but sit around and wait for the storm to pass."*
- *"The most overwhelming thing for me is washing my hair, and the longest I've left it was over three months. I knew I had to wash it, I could feel the grease, but I was just too mentally and emotionally drained to do so."*
- *"Literally everything is overwhelming when you have depression apart from staying in bed."*

Quotes About What It Actually Means When People with Depression Say *"I Can't ..."*

As we have said, unfortunately, when someone with depression says *"I can't ... ,"* it is often interpreted as *"I won't ... ."* However, according to members of The Depression Project's community, when someone with depression says *"I can't ... ,"* what it actually means is

- *"When I'm in a depressive episode and say that I can't do something, it means that I don't have the mental or physical energy to do it."*
- *"It means that I'm spent. It means I'm running on less than fumes and can't physically, mentally, or emotionally will myself to do anything."*
- *"It means that I'm so exhausted and that my body is so heavy that it takes all of my energy just to get out of bed to use the bathroom. Anything beyond that, I can't do right now."*

- *"When I say I can't do something, it means that all of my energy and strength is already being used up just trying to survive."*
- *"It means that depression has destroyed me and left me without any confidence in myself. When you don't believe you can, then you can't."*
- *"'I can't' for me means 'I am broken, and I need some time to mend.'"*
- *"Most people don't understand that when you're being suffocated by depression, even the simplest things feel like climbing a mountain. It's not that I'm being lazy or procrastinating when I say that I can't do something — it's just that depression is draining all of my energy, all of my self-belief, all of my mental and physical strength, and all of my ability to be able to think clearly. In this state, I really can't do anything."*
- *"I say 'I can't' when I just don't have the mental, emotional, or physical energy to do anything but the bare minimum to get by. That's why exercise stops happening, the diet goes bad, the house gets messy, important work tasks go undone, and on and on and on."*
- *"If you can crawl out of depression's hole just enough so that you can get some kind of normal life back, then you have to always guard against slipping back into it again. Sometimes saying 'I can't' is simply managing your own boundaries to stay well."*
- *"Me saying 'I can't' means that I'm at the end of my rope and have nothing left of me to give. It means I barely got this far today, and that I can't face going any further."*
- *"For me, 'I can't' means that I can't do one additional task beyond those that MUST be done right now to survive. It means that I literally only have the energy to do the bare minimum."*

What We Encourage You to Do if Someone You Know with Depression Tells You *"I Can't ..."*

If someone you know who has depression tells you *"I can't ... ,"* please understand that even though whatever they are saying they cannot do might be very simple and easy for *you* to do, given all of the debilitating symptoms of depression that they are dealing with, it is extremely overwhelming and challenging for *them* to do. Consequently, rather than judging them, criticizing them, putting them down, and/or calling them *"lazy,"* please try your best to do the following:

- Be gentle and compassionate toward them instead.
- If you are willing and able to, then offer to help them with any of the tasks that, due to their "depression tiredness," their concentration difficulties and/or their negative thoughts that are sabotaging their confidence, they are telling you that they cannot do right now. After all, when someone with depression is in this state, then lending them a helping hand is a wonderful way in which you can support them.

What We Encourage You to Do if You Have Depression Yourself and Can Relate to Saying *"I Can't ..."*

If you have depression and can relate to one or more of the quotes we shared about what people with depression actually mean when they say *"I can't,"* then first, we hope you can take some comfort in knowing that you are not alone, and that it is very, *very* common to find it extremely difficult to function when you are fighting depression.

Second, because *"I can't ..."* is unfortunately often misinterpreted as *"I won't ..."* by people who have never experienced depression themselves, then to try to overcome the "language barrier" that this phrase can give rise to, we encourage you to do the following:

- Try your best to clarify *why* you *"can't"* right now to the person you are talking to.
- Ask them what you would like from them in this moment.

For example, rather than just saying *"I can't ... ,"* you could instead expand on this by saying something like the following:

- *"I can't do the dishes right now, because I'm feeling extremely depressed and don't have the physical or the mental energy to do anything on top of just trying to survive. If you would be willing to help me out and do them for me, then I would be extremely grateful, and if not, I'll get to them when I'm out of 'survival mode.'"*

- *"Right now, my depression is making me feel so exhausted and broken that I can't get out of bed. Could you please just give me some space to rest and recharge until I feel better?"*

Expanding on *"I can't ..."* in this way can help the person you are talking to better understand what you are actually going through, and as a result, it is less likely that they will put you down, criticize you, and/or call you *"lazy"* for not doing something.

Next: What People with Depression Actually Mean When They Say *"I'm Busy"*

Now that we have explained what people with depression actually mean when they say *"I can't ... ,"* whenever you are ready, we encourage you to move onto Chapter 6, where we will focus on the phrase *"I'm busy"* – which when misunderstood, can unfortunately lead to friends and family members feeling very upset toward their loved one with depression.

6

What People with Depression Actually Mean When They Say *"I'm Busy"*

When someone with depression says *"I'm busy"* at the opportunity to spend time with a loved one – particularly if they do so repeatedly to the point where it becomes a pattern of behavior – it is common for their loved ones to consequently conclude something negative about that person and/or the state of their relationship. In particular, here are some common examples of these negative conclusions:

- *"I'm not important enough for them to make time for me."*
- *"There are many other things they would rather do than spend time with me."*
- *"They're avoiding me."*
- *"They don't care about me."*
- *"We're not as close as we used to be."*

However, as we often hear from members of The Depression Project's community, telling their friends and family members *"I'm busy"* is a common excuse people with depression turn to in order to *socially withdraw and be by themselves* – as a way of dealing with the significant impact that their depression is having on them. With that in mind, we would like to share with you a variety of responses from members of our community when we asked them what they actually mean when they say *"I'm busy."*

What People with Depression Actually Mean When They Say *"I'm Busy"*

- *"I'm so exhausted that I don't have any energy to interact with other people right now."*
- *"I feel too overwhelmed and drained to be able to do anything."*
- *"I can't meet because I am at war with my mind and feel numb to the world around me."*
- *"I don't have the energy to come."*
- *"My schedule is free, but my head is so full of negative thoughts, pain, and hurt that I can't meet up with anyone."*
- *"I am not able to get out of bed."*
- *"I feel so overwhelmed with everything right now, and I really can't handle a single other thing. Even just deciding what to wear will be too much for me – let alone ironing those clothes, putting on make-up, doing my hair, taking public transport to the venue, talking to people, etcetera."*
- *"I am busy trying to get everything done while I have the energy before I spiral."*
- *"When I say 'I'm busy,' it means that I'm probably taking time for self-care."*
- *"Right now, my body and mind won't let me do anything."*
- *"I am busy sleeping to escape my depression."*
- *"I don't have enough energy to go out and pretend that I'm 'fine.'"*
- *"I can't function properly right now and don't want you to see that."*
- *"None of the clothes I would wear to meet people socially are clean, and I don't have the energy to wash them."*

- *"I can't muster up the energy to be around people, even if they mean a lot to me."*
- *"I am busy surviving."*

Our Advice for How to React if Someone You Know with Depression Socially Withdraws by Telling You *"I'm Busy"*

Avoid Jumping to Conclusions

If a loved one with depression turns down one or more opportunities to meet with you because they are *"busy,"* please do not automatically jump to the conclusion that they are telling you *"I'm busy"* because, for example, they do not think you are *"important enough"* to make time for, because there are *"many other things they would rather be doing than spending time with you,"* because they are *"avoiding you,"* because they *"don't care about you,"* and/or because you are *"not as close as you used to be."* After all, as the quotes that we just shared with you show, them saying *"I'm busy"* could just mean that they do not feel up to meeting with you in the way you are suggesting because they are currently too consumed with the symptoms of their depression.

Propose an Alternative Suggestion That Does Not Require as Much Energy

If possible, we encourage you to follow up your original suggestion of what to do with your loved one with depression with a second suggestion that requires less energy and effort for them. This is because, for example, although they might feel far too "depression tired" to go on a hike, to a concert, or to a crowded bar with you, they might feel up to quietly watching a movie with you, or to lying down on their couch and playing video games with you.

Respect Their Boundaries

If they also turn down your follow-up suggestion, then because they might well be going through an awful lot in that moment, instead of trying to pressure them into changing their mind and doing something with you, we encourage you to respect their boundaries and abide by their wishes.

Do Not Stop Inviting Them

Even if your loved one with depression repeatedly turns down your invitations to meet with you, we still encourage you to continue reaching out and inviting them to do so. Although this might seem pointless, continuing to reach out to your loved one with depression who is socially withdrawing still serves the very important purpose of showing them that

- You care.
- They are still important to you.
- You have not given up on them.
- They will be warmly welcomed whenever they are ready to come out of withdrawal and re-engage with the world again.

And, when someone is in a depressive episode, then, as we so often hear from members of our community, knowing this can mean the absolute world to them (particularly when, sadly, some of their other loved ones might have given up and stopped contacting them).

Try to Still Engage with Your Loved One with Depression in Whatever Other Small, Nice Ways You Can

Last, if your loved one with depression does continuously avoid opportunities to meet, we encourage you to try your best to still engage with them in whatever other small, nice ways you can. For example, you could

- Message them the highlights of a sporting event you both like, and tell or ask them something about it.
- Ask them if they have seen a popular new television series, and invite them to watch it with you online.

- Share something that made you think of them (such as a picture from a previous trip you took together).
- Forward them a funny video or meme that made you laugh.
- Link them to an article that they might find interesting.
- Invite them to play a game with you online.
- Order them a bouquet of flowers, a box of chocolates, or their favorite meal to be delivered to their home.
- Remind them of something funny they once did.
- Ask them their opinion on something (such as about a new outfit you are considering buying, about the new person you have agreed to go on a date with, or anything else that they might have an interest in).
- Send them an uplifting, heartfelt card.
- Remind them that you are always there for them if they ever need anything.

These are not only nice ways of keeping in touch with your loved one with depression, but they also serve the very important purpose of giving them a boost when they are in a depressive episode, and of helping them feel like they are not alone – both of which they will no doubt be very grateful for.

Our Advice for People Who Have Depression and Say *"I'm Busy"* as an Excuse to Socially Withdraw

Try to Engage with Your Loved Ones in Whatever Ways You Can Manage

Although socially withdrawing by saying *"I'm busy"* is very understandable when you are in a depressive episode, as we often hear from members of our community, doing so can leave you feeling lonely, isolated, and even more depressed. And, if you can relate, then when possible, we encourage you to *try to engage with other people in whatever small, manageable ways that you can.*

After all, although many forms of social interaction might feel too overwhelming when you are deep in a depressive episode, this does not necessarily mean that you cannot engage with anybody *at all*. For example:

- If you have a group of 10 friends who usually get together, then if meeting *all* of them in a busy environment feels like too much, then perhaps you could reach out to *one* of those friends who has shown themselves to be empathetic and compassionate, and suggest to meet them somewhere much more quiet.
- Or, if meeting up with them face-to-face feels too overwhelming, then perhaps you could talk over text message.
- Or, if talking in any capacity is not something you feel you can manage, then perhaps you could do a more passive activity together online – such as, as we mentioned, playing a game or watching a television series together.

If you are able to interact with other people in the small, manageable ways that you can, then it can make a big difference toward helping you feel much less lonely, much less isolated, and consequently less depressed.

Try to Be Transparent About the Real Reasons Why You Are Declining an Opportunity to Spend Time with Someone

As we have said, when you decline an opportunity to spend time with someone by telling them *"I'm busy"* – particularly if you do so repeatedly – that person might then jump to the conclusion that, for example, you do not think they are *"important enough"* to make time for, you have *"many other things you would rather be doing than spending time with them,"* you are *"avoiding them,"* you *"don't care about them,"* and/or that the two of you are *"not as close as you used to be."* Consequently, to try to prevent this from happening and be better understood instead, we encourage you to express to the person you are talking to the *real reasons* why you are declining an opportunity to spend time with them. For example:

- If someone invites you to a party, then rather than declining by saying *"I'm busy,"* you could instead tell them: *"Usually I would*

*really love to go, but my depression has drained my energy this week,
so unfortunately I'll have to pass."*

- If someone suggests meeting for dinner, then rather than
  declining by saying *"I'm busy,"* you could instead tell them:
  *"Can I take a raincheck? My depression's sunk in and I feel too over-
  whelmed to do anything tonight, but I'd love to catch up with you once
  I'm feeling better."*

As we said, responding in a more informative way like so is likely
to help your loved ones understand you better, and as a result, they
will be less likely to jump to negative conclusions about you and/or
their relationship with you.

Next: What People with Depression Actually Mean When They Say *"I Want to Go Home"*

In this chapter

- We talked about the "language barrier" that the phrase *"I'm
  busy"* can give rise to, and explained what people with depression often actually mean when they say this.
- We shared some effective ways for supporters to respond when
  someone they care about with depression tells them *"I'm busy."*
- We encouraged people with depression to try to reach out to
  others in whatever small, manageable ways they can when they
  are in a period of social withdrawal, and to be transparent about
  the real reasons why they are choosing not to spend time with
  someone they care about.

Next, in Chapter 7. we are going to focus on yet another phrase
that is often misunderstood by friends and family of people with
depression: *"I want to go home."*

7

What People with Depression Actually Mean When They Say *"I Want to Go Home"*

Rather than socially withdrawing by saying *"I'm busy,"* there will of course also most likely be times when people with depression leave their home to spend time with others. However, in these situations, for a variety of reasons, they might want to return home earlier (and sometimes *much* earlier) than the people they are with would expect them to. And unfortunately, when this happens, it is common for those people to not understand the reasons why. Depending on the situation, this might have the following consequences:

- It might cause those people to feel annoyed with their loved one with depression, and/or think that they are "rude" and/or "selfish" (particularly if their loved one with depression wanting to go home much earlier than expected ruins their plans).
- It might cause those people to feel offended and/or hurt by their loved one with depression (particularly if they had gone to a lot of effort to plan something that their loved one with depression now wants to leave earlier than expected from, and/or if what their loved one with depression wants to leave early from is a significant event like their birthday celebration, for example, which is very important to them).
- It might cause those people to feel that their loved one with depression is "boring" or a "party pooper" (particularly if, for example, their loved one with depression says *"I want to go home"* in the middle of a party or another lively event where everyone else is having fun).

However, when someone with depression says *"I want to go home"* earlier than the people they are with would expect them to, it is not because they are *"rude," "selfish,"* or *"boring,"* for example. Rather, according to members of The Depression Project's community, when someone with depression says *"I want to go home,"* what is really going through their mind is

- *"I am completely and utterly exhausted. I've tried my best to carry on and push through because I don't want to disappoint anyone, but I am drained. I am like a phone that is out of batteries. I need to go home to rest and recharge."*
- *"I can only mask my depression for so long, and it's getting very close to the time when I'll no longer be able to keep it up. I want to leave and go home so that no one is around when I break down."*
- *"My depression is setting in and taking hold of me again. I need to be home in my safe place to cope with all the symptoms that I'm suddenly now dealing with."*
- *"Continuing to engage with others is just too overwhelming. I wish it wasn't – believe me, I'd love nothing more than to be free of my*

depression and have the energy to talk to everyone and have a blast. But I'm done. I'm spent. Even making small talk has become too much for me."

- "Everything around me is too overstimulating. I need to go home where it's quiet so that I can process my thoughts."

- "My depression has become too much to cope with. I just want to be at home where I can collapse on my bed and bawl my eyes out."

- "I feel like I'm stopping others from having fun and that no one wants me here."

- "I feel under too much pressure to have fun and be in a good mood. Being around other people who are so happy and joyous when I'm miserable on the inside makes me feel out of place, and feeling out of place makes me even more depressed."

- "My social battery is completely dead. Continuing to talk and be around others has become too overwhelming for me."

- "I am just too tired and broken to stay. I wish I wasn't, because I'd really been looking forward to seeing you, but my depression is weighing me down so unbelievably much and is too heavy for me to keep on carrying. I'm so sorry. I really am sorry."

What We Encourage You to Do if You Have Depression Yourself and You Can Relate to Saying *"I Want to Go Home"* Early

If you have depression and when you are out with others, you often feel the urge to return home earlier than other people would expect you to, then we would like to share the following three pieces of advice that we think you will find helpful in navigating this issue moving forward.

Try to Set Accurate Expectations in Advance

Your friends and family members might feel annoyed, offended, and/or hurt if when you are with them, you tell them you want to go home earlier than they had expected you to leave. However, if prior to meeting, you are able to tell them what you are going through and adjust their expectations about how much time you are likely to be able to spend with them, then

- It can help prevent them from feeling annoyed, offended, and/ or hurt when you tell them that you want to go home.
- Because you will likely be less nervous that you telling them *"I want to go home"* is going to result in them feeling "annoyed," "offended," and/or "hurt," it can also help to make you feel more comfortable when you are actually with them. This will not only make your time with them more enjoyable, but by "taking some of the pressure off," it also might result in you having the capacity to end up spending longer with them than you otherwise would have.

With these objectives in mind, in order to set these accurate expectations, you could, for example, try the following:

- If someone invites you to their birthday party, tell them beforehand: *"I would really like to come and celebrate your birthday with you, but just so you know, I might need to leave early. Unfortunately, my depression has been flaring up this week and I've been feeling really tired as a result, so I have nowhere near as much energy as I otherwise would. But, I am looking forward to coming to your party and staying for as long as I can manage!"*
- If someone suggests spending the afternoon shopping at a busy mall together, tell them beforehand: *"That would be fun, but I'm not sure I'll be able to last the whole afternoon, because if I spend too long in really busy environments, I end up feeling too overstimulated and overwhelmed, which is bad for my depression. So, could we instead just go for an hour or two?"*

Of course, it might not always be possible to set accurate expectations in advance like this – particularly because depression's symptoms can set in abruptly, which can mean that you might feel the sudden urge to go home in situations in which you had not previously expected you would want to leave early. However, when it is possible for you to do so, we think you will find setting accurate expectations a helpful method of preventing your friends and family members from feeling annoyed, offended, and/or hurt by you going home earlier than you otherwise would have because of your depression.

Try to Explain the Reason(s) Why You Want to Go Home

In addition to trying to set accurate expectations in advance, another helpful strategy to prevent your friends and family members from feeling annoyed, offended, and/or hurt by you going home early is for you to explain the reasons why you feel the urge to do so. For example, rather than saying *"I want to go home now"* or some variation thereof, you could instead perhaps say:

- *"I'd love to be able to stay longer, but unfortunately my depression is sinking in, so I really should go home and do what I have to do to cope with it."*
- *"It's been great seeing you, but I need to leave, I'm afraid. My depression's been flaring up lately and whenever this happens I feel really exhausted, so I'd better go home and rest."*

If you do not feel comfortable explaining your reason(s) for wanting to go home in these ways when you are about to leave – for example, because you are worried you will not express yourself in the way you want to, or because there are a lot of people around and you do not feel comfortable mentioning your depression in front of them – then you might find it easier to explain your reason(s) for leaving at some point *after* you have already left (such as by, for example, sending a message the following day). Either way, if the people you were with understand that you wanted to go home because of the debilitating impact that your depression was having on you – as opposed to anything to do with them personally – then they are much less likely to feel annoyed, offended, and/or hurt by you leaving early.

Be Compassionate with Yourself

When you return home earlier than when other people had expected you to or than when you would have wanted to, then if you are like many people with depression, you might use it as a reason to be self-critical, and think negative thoughts such as, for example:

- *"I'm not as much fun as I used to be."*
- *"I'm so boring for going home early."*
- *"I'm such a loser for always being the first person to leave and go home."*

And, if you can relate, then anytime you find yourself having these negative thoughts:

1. We encourage you to remind yourself that, when you feel the urge to go home early, *you are not alone* because, as the quotes we previously shared with you show, this is very common when you have depression.

2. We encourage you to remind yourself that in addition to being extremely common, it is also extremely understandable. After all, when you are being weighed down by depression's intense, debilitating symptoms, it is perfectly natural that your "social battery" will run out before the "social battery" of other people who are *not* being weighed down by all of these symptoms.

3. Instead of criticizing yourself for wanting to go home early, we encourage you to give yourself credit for leaving your home to socialize in the first place, and then focus your attention on resting, soothing yourself, and practicing self-care. If you are able to be kind and compassionate with yourself in this way instead of being self-critical, it is likely going to help your batteries recharge quicker than they otherwise would, as well as contribute to pulling you out of a depressive episode as opposed to keeping you trapped in it.

Our Advice for Supporters When Their Loved One with Depression Tells Them *"I Want to Go Home"*

As the quotes that we previously shared with you from members of The Depression Project's community indicate, if someone you care about with depression tells you *"I want to go home"* earlier than you had expected them to, then it is a sign that at that point in time, their depression is likely taking its toll on them. And, in light of this, we would now like to share four suggestions for how to respond in this instance.

Try to Be Compassionate Instead of Judging Them

Rather than judging them for leaving early and concluding that they are *"rude," "selfish,"* or *"boring,"* for example, please try your best to be compassionate, and to not hold the impact of their depression against them when they are doing their best to cope with it.

Avoid Pressuring Them to Stay

If your loved one with depression specifically tells you that the reason they want to go home is because they feel *"not wanted"* or because they feel that they are *"bringing the mood down"* – which are negative thoughts people with depression might be liable to think – then they will likely appreciate it if you reassure them that this is not the case and encourage them to stay. However, if they say that they want to go home *without* explicitly providing this as a reason why, rather than trying to convince them to stay, we encourage you to respect and abide by their wishes. After all, as the quotes we shared from members of The Depression Project's community show, when someone is battling depression, there are several very valid reasons why it might indeed be in their best interests to go home. And, for this reason, we encourage you not to stand in the way of them doing so.

Offer Your Support if You Can

We encourage you to ask your loved one with depression if there is anything you can do to help them, support them, or to make their life easier, and reiterate that you are there for them if they need anything.

Check In with Them Later

Last, sometime after your loved one with depression has gone home, we also encourage you to check in on them – for example, by sending them a message along the lines of *"I hope you're OK. Please let me know if you need anything."* Although your loved one might be feeling too depressed, tired, or drained to take you up on your offer or to even check their phone and respond to your message, the fact that you are reaching out to them and offering to help will still likely mean a lot to them, and contribute to them feeling supported, cared for, and not alone.

Next: What People with Depression Actually Mean When They Say *"I Don't Care"*

Now that we have explained what people with depression actually mean when they say *"I want to go home,"* whenever you are ready, we encourage you to move onto Chapter 8, where we will focus on yet another commonly said phrase that can cause conflict between people with depression and their loved ones: *"I don't care."*

8

What People with Depression Actually Mean When They Say *"I Don't Care"*

When someone has depression, something they might say quite frequently is the phrase *"I don't care."* In particular:

- They might say *"I don't care"* in response to being asked for their input on something – such as when their partner asks them *"what would you like to do on date night this week?"* or when their sibling asks them *"what gift would you like me to get you for your birthday this year?"*
- People with depression might say *"I don't care"* in response to being asked to make a decision between multiple options – such as when their partner asks them *"would you prefer that I cook us spaghetti bolognaise or a chicken stir fry for dinner?"* or

when their friend asks them *"would you rather watch the basketball game on television tonight or reruns of* Friends *again?"*

- People with depression might say *"I don't care"* in response to someone sharing something with them that they think they will be interested in – such as when their friend is telling them the details of the latest trade that the football team they both support made, and then asking them what they think about it.
- People with depression might say *"I don't care"* (or *"I don't care anymore"*) in the middle of an argument or a difficult conversation.

And, when people with depression say *"I don't care"* to their loved ones in these contexts, then the following can happen:

- It can cause their loved ones to feel upset, offended, and/or hurt (particularly if they are being told *"I don't care"* in response to something that is important to them, or if they are being told *"I don't care"* in response to something they are putting a lot of thought, care, and effort into).
- It can cause them to feel as if their loved one with depression does not care about *them* (particularly if they are told *"I don't care"* repeatedly about something [or more than one thing] that is important to them).

However, when someone with depression says *"I don't care,"* it is *not* because they are trying to *"upset," "offend,"* or *"hurt"* their loved ones, and it certainly does *not* mean that they *"don't care about them."* Rather, according to members of The Depression Project's community, when someone with depression says *"I don't care,"* what they can actually mean is the following:

- *"I am too consumed with depression to be able to deal with this right now."*
- *"I am absolutely exhausted and finding it impossible to concentrate, so I'm really not in the right frame of mind to make any decisions."*

- *"My depression is so bad that I have shut down. I am numb. I am emotionless when I'm in this state, and even though I would usually care about this, right now, I just don't care."*
- *"I feel so empty, broken, and lacking in hope that nothing seems to matter anymore, so who cares? What difference will it make?"*
- *"I am so overwhelmed that I can't add anything more to my thoughts. I know what you're asking me is only a basic question that I should be able to think about and answer within a few seconds, but even that is too much for me right now."*
- *"I don't have the energy or the strength to care right now. That doesn't mean what you're asking me or telling me isn't important; it means my depression is too strong right now for me to think about it."*
- *"I am so focused on surviving that I can't deal with anything else right now."*
- *"It's too hard to make a decision. I have brain fog. My mind is too clouded with negative thoughts and I'm in too much pain to be able to think clearly."*
- *"Usually I would care about this, but my depression is so bad right now that it's suffocating my interest and enthusiasm in everything."*
- *"I'm numb and don't care about anything, least of all myself right now."*

Our Advice for Supporters When Their Loved One with Depression Tells Them *"I Don't Care"*

As these quotes show, when someone with depression says *"I don't care,"* then it is an indication of the following:

- They are currently being significantly affected by depression's symptoms.
- As a result, they currently lack the capacity to give their input on something, make a decision about something, or feel as much emotion toward something as they otherwise would.

In light of this, if someone with depression tells you *"I don't care,"* we would like to share the following suggestions about how to respond.

Try Not to Take Their Lack of Care Personally

When a loved one with depression tells you *"I don't care,"* although it is understandable that you might be upset, offended, and/or hurt by this and feel that they do not care about you, we encourage you to remind yourself that them saying *"I don't care"* is a reflection of their depression significantly affecting them at that time – *not* of their true feelings toward you or whatever they are saying *"I don't care"* in response to. Or, to paraphrase one of the previous quotes in particular, we encourage you to remind yourself that *usually, your loved one with depression would care about what you are talking about, but right now, their depression is so intense that it is suffocating their interest and enthusiasm in everything.*

Refrain from Continuing to Try to Solicit Input, a Decision, or a Response from Them

If your loved one is too consumed with their depression to be able to care about something you are telling or asking them, we encourage you to forego continuing to seek input, a decision, or a response from them – because doing so is likely to make them feel even more overwhelmed, even more exhausted, to agitate them, and/or to make them feel even worse. Instead, please consider the following suggestions:

- If they are saying *"I don't care"* in response to you asking for their input or for them to make a decision about something that is relatively minor, we encourage you to go ahead and make the decision yourself.
- If they are saying *"I don't care"* in response to you asking for their input or for them to make a decision about something that is relatively important and ideally requires their involvement, then if possible, we encourage you to wait until they have more capacity to be involved, and then try to discuss it with them again then. Alternatively, if a deadline exists which requires that decision to be made right then and there, then we encourage you to suggest what you think the best way to proceed is,

and then ask them if they have any objections to this. Unless they object, we encourage you to proceed in this way.

■ If they are saying *"I don't care"* in response to you sharing something with them that you think they will be interested in, we encourage you to wait a while and then try again later – at which point, they will hopefully be in a better headspace to engage in what you are telling them.

■ If they are saying *"I don't care"* in the middle of an argument or a difficult conversation when it seems that they have reached the end of their tether, we encourage you to give them some time to recharge their batteries, and then try to peacefully resolve the matter with them then.

Our Advice for You if You Have Depression Yourself and Can Relate to Saying *"I Don't Care"*

If you are in the habit of saying *"I don't care"* when you are being significantly weighed down by your depression, we encourage you to:

■ Explain *why* you *"don't care"* to the person you are talking to.
■ Communicate what you would like from them in that moment.

For example, rather than just saying *"I don't care,"* you could instead expand on this by saying something along the lines of

■ *"I'm sorry, but I'm way too consumed with my depression to be able to think properly about this right now. Could you please just make a decision for us?"*
■ *"To be honest, I feel so overwhelmed right now that I just don't have the capacity for this. Can we please talk about it later?"*
■ *"I'm feeling numb now, so I'm finding it really hard to care about anything. Can we please discuss it when I feel better?"*

Expanding on the phrase *"I don't care"* in this way can help the person you are speaking with understand you better than they would if you only say *"I don't care"* – and as a result, they are much less likely to

- Be upset, offended, and/or hurt.
- Feel that you do not care about them.
- Continue trying to solicit input, a decision, or a response from you that in that moment is beyond your capacity to give them.

Next: What People with Depression Actually Mean When They Say *"I'm Not Hungry"*

In addition to *"I don't care,"* yet another phrase that can cause confusion and conflict between people with depression and those around them is *"I'm not hungry."* So, we will focus on this phrase next in Chapter 9.

9

What People with Depression Actually Mean When They Say *"I'm Not Hungry"*

When fighting depression, some people's relationship to food will be very different to that of other people's. After all, as we mentioned in Chapter 1 when we identified some of depression's most common symptoms, some people will turn to "comfort eating" to try to give themselves some temporary relief from the severity of their symptoms. However, as we also touched on in Chapter 1, it is also common for people with depression to constantly say *"I'm not hungry"* and not eat anywhere near as much as they otherwise would. And, when it comes to this latter situation in particular, it can result in various misunderstandings with the people around them – most notably, with those who live with them, and/or those who would customarily share at least some of their meals with them. In particular, according to members of The Depression Project's community, some common examples of this misunderstanding include

- Friends and family of someone with depression might assume that them saying *"I'm not hungry"* means the exact same thing as it does when somebody who *doesn't* have depression says *"I'm not hungry"*: that they have eaten fairly recently, and that because they are therefore full, they would like to wait a while before eating again.

- Friends and family might think that their loved one with depression is being unnecessarily "fussy" and "picky" with their food when they say *"I'm not hungry"* – which can cause them to feel frustrated toward them.

- They might also be frustrated with their loved one with depression if they conclude that they are being *"overdramatic"* and/or *"just looking for attention and sympathy"* when they refuse to eat (particularly if it has been a long time since they have previously eaten).

- If they have put a lot of effort into preparing a meal for their loved one with depression and have been told *"I'm not hungry"* in response, then they might think that their loved one with depression is being *"rude"* and/or *"ungrateful"* – which can cause them to feel annoyed and/or offended.

- Because sharing a meal together is a common bonding experience, if their loved one with depression tells them *"I'm not hungry"* anytime they suggest eating together, then it can cause them to feel rejected, and less close to their loved one with depression.

- Friends and family of someone with depression might also feel as if they have "failed" – for example, if they try to cook a nice meal for their loved one with depression or invite them to a restaurant with lots of delicious dishes, only to then be told *"I'm not hungry."*

Consequently, because saying *"I'm not hungry"* and declining to eat can give rise to so much misunderstanding and often conflict between someone with depression and the people around them, to shed some light on this issue, we posed the following question to our community members:

> *"Aside from the obvious explanation, what do people with depression actually mean when they say 'I'm not hungry'?"*

Next, we would like to share some of the responses with you.

Aside from the Obvious Explanation, What Do People with Depression Actually Mean When They Say *"I'm Not Hungry"*?

- *"I don't have any appetite. I never do when I'm deep in depression."*
- *"I'm too exhausted and overwhelmed to be bothered choosing what to eat, then cooking or preparing it, then eating it."*
- *"Depression has robbed me of interest in everything I used to enjoy – including food."*
- *"Depression and stress is suppressing my appetite right now."*
- *"Even the thought of eating is nauseating to me. I'm sorry, but I just can't do it."*
- *"I'm at war with too many symptoms of depression to be able to stop and recognize my own needs right now."*
- *"I have no energy to make myself a meal, and honestly, I don't even care anymore whether I'm healthy or not. I'm too depressed. What's the point?"*
- *"It requires too much energy to have to decide what to eat, remember how to make it, and then sit down to eat it. I can hardly get out of bed, so I'm too exhausted for all of that."*
- *"I have no appetite. When I'm depressed, food makes me queasy. It makes me sick."*
- *"When I'm depressed, I feel numb. My senses are dulled, including my sense of taste. When this is the case, eating becomes much less interesting."*

- *"I have zero desire to eat. I will puke if I do."*
- *"For me, it means that I don't care enough about myself to nourish myself at the moment."*
- *"I'm so stuck in my head and so disconnected from my body that I struggle to engage in anything and everything, including eating."*
- *"When I say 'I'm not hungry,' it means that I'm too overwhelmed to even think about making myself something to eat, even though deep down, I know it'll only take me five minutes and will do me good."*

Our Advice for You if You Don't Have Depression Yourself, but if Someone You Know Does and Often Tells You *"I'm Not Hungry"*

When someone with depression says *"I'm not hungry,"* then, of course, it might mean the same thing it usually does when someone who does *not* have depression says that they are not hungry: they have no appetite because they have eaten recently, so they would like to wait a while before eating again. However, as the quotes from members of The Depression Project's community that we just shared with you indicate, when someone with depression says *"I'm not hungry,"* it is also possible that

- Because of their depression, they have no appetite (as we mentioned in Chapter 1, this is a symptom of depression).
- Because of their depression, they feel nauseous (as we also mentioned in Chapter 1, this is another symptom of depression).
- Organizing a meal for themselves is too overwhelming.
- Due to feeling numb because of their depression, their taste-buds are dulled, and they consequently have minimal interest in eating.

For these reasons, we would now like to share with you the following advice.

Try to Avoid Jumping to Conclusions

First and foremost, we really encourage you to try to avoid jumping to any of the conclusions that we mentioned at the start of this chapter. After all, as the quotes we shared with you indicate

- These conclusions *might not be correct* (when it comes to the assumption that your loved one with depression is saying *"I'm not hungry"* because they have eaten recently and are therefore full).
- These conclusions are *almost certainly incorrect* (when it comes to the conclusions surrounding your loved one with depression being *"fussy,"* *"picky,"* *"overdramatic,"* *"rude,"* *"ungrateful,"* or *"just looking for attention and sympathy"*).

Try to Gently Encourage / Make It Easier for Your Loved One with Depression to Eat (but Please Do Not Pressure Them to Eat and/or Take It Personally if They Still Do Not)

If your loved one with depression frequently tells you *"I'm not hungry"* and you do not believe they are eating as much as they should be, then if you want to try to help them, we encourage you to make it as easy as possible for them to eat. For example, you could perhaps

- Prepare them a nutritious meal so that they do not have to do so themselves when they are feeling exhausted and overwhelmed (and if you are able to, it will also likely be helpful for them if you cook multiple servings of that meal and then put it in the fridge so that for future meals, all your loved one with depression needs to do is heat it up).
- Alternatively (or as well as), you could make a trip to the grocery store on their behalf, and buy them the following:
  - Meals they can eat that require little-to-no preparation, such as microwaveable meals, premade salads, and/or cereal for breakfast.
  - Snacks that do not require any preparation, such as fresh fruit, yogurt, and muesli bars (additionally, snacks are also great for people with depression to have on hand as a replacement for a complete meal if they have a limited appetite).
  - Meal replacement drinks (such as smoothies) if your loved one with depression is having difficulty stomaching solid food.

In saying this, though, as helpful as these supportive acts can be for your loved one with depression, we also encourage you not to pressure or force them into eating – because at that point in time, they truly might not have the capacity to do so. Additionally, we also encourage you to try your best not to take it personally or think that you have *"failed"* if, despite your best efforts, your loved one with depression still says *"I'm not hungry"* and declines to eat (or does not eat very much of, for example, a meal you prepared for them). After all, the effort you put in likely still made them feel loved, supported, and cared for (even if they are too depressed to be able to show their gratitude to you). Not only that but sometime in the future, they eventually will eat – at which point, they will also likely be relieved and grateful that you made it easier for them to do so.

Look for Other Nice Ways to Have Shared Experiences Together

As we have mentioned, because sharing a meal with someone is a common bonding experience, if your loved one with depression tells you *"I'm not hungry"* anytime you suggest eating with them, then it might leave you feeling rejected and disconnected from them. And, if you can relate

- We encourage you to remind yourself that your loved one with depression is not trying to reject you. Rather, due to their depression, they are just not in a position to be able to eat with you right now.
- We encourage you to try to replace eating together with one or more alternative activities that might be easier for them to engage in, and that still contribute to you feeling close and connected with them. In practice, these activities could include, for example, watching television together, playing video games, listening to music, doing a puzzle, going for a walk in nature, and/or taking a drive somewhere.

What We Encourage You to Do if You Have Depression Yourself and Can Relate to Telling People *"I'm Not Hungry"* and Declining to Eat

If telling your friends and family members *"I'm not hungry"* and declining to eat is something you can relate to doing, please know that you are not alone – as evidenced by all of the quotes that we shared with you. In saying that, however, to overcome the "language barrier" that saying *"I'm not hungry"* can give rise to, we would like to offer a couple of suggestions that we think will be helpful.

Try to Communicate to the Person You Are Talking to the Reason(s) Why You Are Not Hungry

As we have said, when you tell someone *"I'm not hungry"* and then decline to eat, they might jump to the conclusion that, for example, you are just being *"fussy," "picky," "overdramatic," "rude," "ungrateful,"* or *"just looking for attention and sympathy."* Consequently, to try to prevent this from happening and be better understood instead, we encourage you to express to the person you are talking to the reason(s) *why* you do not want to eat. For example:

- If someone invites you to a restaurant to eat with them, you could respond with the following: *"I'd normally love to, but my depression has set in and is suppressing my appetite. Can I take a raincheck for when I'm feeling better and my hunger is back?"*
- If someone cooks you a meal, you could say, *"I really appreciate you doing this for me, but I need to wait a while before eating. Unfortunately, nausea is a symptom of depression, and right now, the thought of eating is making me queasy."*

As we've said, responding in a more informative way like so is likely to help your loved ones understand you better, and as a result, chances are they will be less likely to jump to negative conclusions.

Think of Alternative Ways That You Can Connect with Your Loved Ones

As we also mentioned, if sharing a meal together is one of the ways that you have customarily connected with the people you care about, when your appetite is diminished, try connecting with them in alternative ways that feel safe, comfortable, and manageable for you.

Next: What People with Depression Actually Mean When They Say *"I'm Having a Good Day"*

Now that we have explained what people with depression actually mean when they say *"I'm not hungry,"* whenever you are ready, we encourage you to move onto Chapter 10, where we will focus on the phrase *"I'm having a good day"* – which unfortunately, is sometimes misconstrued in a way that can result in people with depression being accused of *"faking it," "making it up," "looking for attention,"* or *"just being overdramatic."*

10

What People with Depression Actually Mean When They Say *"I'm Having a Good Day"*

A big misconception surrounding depression is that if someone struggles with this illness, then it means they are miserable 100% of the time. Consequently, as we often hear from members of The Depression Project's community, if they say they are having a *"good day,"* then it can lead their friends and family members to falsely conclude

1. They were previously *"faking it," "making it up," "looking for attention,"* or *"just being overdramatic"* when they said that they struggled with depression.

2. If they did struggle with depression, then they are now recovered – which means that if at any point in the future they
claim to be feeling depressed, then they must be *"faking it,"*
"making it up," "looking for attention," or *"just being overdramatic."*

However, in reality, people with depression can – and almost
certainly will! – have some *"good days,"* in spite of the fact that they
are indeed struggling with depression. And, the reason why is because
*people with depression experience varying intensities of symptoms at different
times* – as opposed to feeling miserable and suffering from the most
extreme form of their symptoms 100% of the time.

If you do not have depression yourself but you know someone
who does, then to help you understand this point better, we would
now like to remind you of the Storm to Sun Framework we discussed
in Chapter 2 – which comprises three different zones that at any point
in time, your loved one with depression might find themselves in.

The Storm Zone

Someone with depression can be said to be in the Storm Zone of the
Storm to Sun Framework when the symptoms of their depression are
severe. In this zone:

- They are usually being bombarded with negative thoughts,
  their negative thoughts are usually at their most negative and
  catastrophic, and they are usually at their most attached to those
  negative thoughts (i.e., more so than at any other time, they
  believe them to be true).
- Emotions like misery, shame, worthlessness, hopelessness, and
  so on are felt more intensely than ever.
- In the Storm Zone, a person's ability to function tends to be
  significantly compromised – to such an extent that fulfilling
  their day-to-day responsibilities can feel unmanageable (and
  often are), and even simple tasks like getting out of bed or
  having a shower, for example, might feel like climbing a
  mountain.

- Faking a smile and pretending to be "OK" might be impossible.
- In the Storm Zone, it is common for someone with depression to feel so miserable, broken, and hopeless that they might be unable to envision the storm ever passing.

The Rain Zone

Someone with depression can be said to be in the Rain Zone when the symptoms of their depression are *moderately intense*. In this zone:

- The storm in their mind has calmed down or not yet started, but it could flare up on short notice.
- Because their symptoms are only moderately severe, they can likely still uphold their responsibilities and carry on with daily life – but they will probably get tired much quicker than they otherwise would.
- Feeling "burned out" is common, and they might be prone to snapping easily.
- Socializing and/or interacting with others – although possible – often feels too draining.

The Cloud Zone

This is when a person with depression's symptoms are *mild*. In this zone:

- They feel more or less "normal" in the sense that their days are only minimally (if at all) affected by depression.
- They are able to function relatively well without becoming easily tired.
- They are much more likely to want to socialize with friends and family and interact with other people.
- In the Cloud Zone, their motivation is at its highest, so they are most able to do the things that they might have been putting off doing while they were in the Storm or Rain Zones.

What It Actually Means When Someone with Depression Says *"I'm Having a Good Day"*

Returning to the point that we made previously, when someone with depression says that they are *"having a good day,"* what it means is that they are most likely in the Cloud Zone of the Storm to Sun Framework (or perhaps the Rain Zone if they had previously been in the Storm Zone for an extended period of time). And, for this reason, if someone you know with depression tells you *"I'm having a good day"*:

1. Please do *not* accuse them of having *"faked it," "made it up," "been looking for attention,"* or *"been overdramatic"* for having previously said that they were struggling with depression. After all, as we've said and as the Storm to Sun Framework highlights, people with depression experience varying intensities of symptoms at different times, as opposed to feeling miserable and suffering from the most extreme form of their symptoms 100% of the time. And, for this reason, it is entirely possible for someone to have a *"good day"* even when they have depression.

2. Additionally, please do not assume that just because someone with depression is having a *"good day,"* that it means they have now *"recovered"* from their depression, and that therefore
   - They will never feel depressed again moving forward.
   - If they ever do claim they are feeling depressed again in the future, that it means they must be *"faking it," "making it up," "looking for attention,"* or *"just being overdramatic."*

After all, to emphasize the point once again, people with depression experience varying intensities of symptoms at different times. And, for this reason, it is entirely possible for someone with depression to – after having a *"good day"* when they are in the Cloud Zone of the Storm to Sun Framework – later find themselves in the Rain or the Storm Zone dealing with moderate or severely intense symptoms of depression.

Next: The Language People with Depression Use That Can Mean They Are Suicidal

In this chapter, we clarified what people with depression actually mean when they say *"I'm having a good day"* – which is one of the many phrases we have looked at in Part I of this book for which there exists a "language barrier" between people with depression and those around them. And, in the next part of this book, we are going to look at a range of additional phrases for which depression's "language barrier" exists as well that, although often dismissed by the people around them, can actually mean that someone with depression is suicidal.

Depression's "Verbal Language Barrier" in the Context of Suicide in Particular

11 | The Language People with Depression Use That Can Mean They Are Suicidal

Tragically, in their fight against depression, it is common for people to feel suicidal – and in the worst of cases, for them to act on these feelings. And, although there is various language that people with depression often use that can indicate to their loved ones that they are feeling suicidal,[1] once again, it is common for a "language barrier" to exist between them, which can result in people with depression who are feeling suicidal experiencing the following:

- Not being properly understood
- Having their feelings dismissed instead of taken seriously and acted on

- Not receiving the help they need, which puts them at greater risk of actually attempting suicide.

In particular, through interacting with many members of The Depression Project's community, we have come to believe that there are two common reasons for this "language barrier":

- Friends and family members of people with depression are not always aware of suicide's *verbal warning signs* – or, put another way, they are not always familiar with the language that people with depression often use that can indicate that they are feeling suicidal.
- Alternatively, they might recognize that the language their loved one with depression is using could *theoretically* be a warning sign that they are feeling suicidal, however, they do not believe that they actually *are* suicidal – and as a result, they do not take what their loved one with depression is telling them anywhere near as seriously as they otherwise would. In particular, this is often because
  - They misinterpret their loved one with depression using this language as them, for example, *"just looking for attention," "just being overdramatic," "just being negative,"* and/or *"just being weak."*
  - They do not believe what their loved one with depression is telling them is *"rational"* or *"factually correct."*
  - They do not believe that what their loved one with depression is going through is *"that bad."*
  - When their loved one with depression uses this language in a lighthearted, humorous way, they misinterpret it as them *"only joking."*

Consequently, to overcome this "language barrier" so people with depression who are feeling suicidal can be properly understood, taken seriously, and treated in a way that helps keep them safe and leads to them receiving the support they need, in this chapter

- We will highlight the language that people with depression often use that warns that they might be feeling suicidal, and explain why this language should be taken seriously by the people around them.
- We will offer some advice to supporters about what they can do if they pick up on their loved one with depression using language that signals that they might be feeling suicidal, in order to
  - Help their loved one with depression remain safe.
  - Help them receive the appropriate level of care and support they need moving forward.

It goes without saying that this is one of the most — if not *the most* — important sections of this book. So, as soon as you are ready, let's get started.

The Language People with Depression Use That Can Mean They Are Suicidal

Although suicide attempts are not always preceded by language that hints that that person might be feeling suicidal, in many cases, they are — which is why it is extremely important that everybody is aware of this language. On that note, we would now like to highlight some common phrases that indicate that a person might be feeling suicidal, as well as explain why their loved ones should take these comments extremely seriously.

Saying "I Want to Give Up"

If someone has been fighting their depression for a very long time — particularly if they feel as if they have done everything in their power to get better and none of their efforts have worked — then they might reach a tipping point where

- They have become conditioned to believe that no matter what they do, they will never beat their depression.
- They have no strength – or desire – left to continue fighting a battle they do not think they can win.

And, when people are feeling overwhelmed with depression's symptoms, defeated and devoid of hope, then they might feel inclined to stop fighting their depression and instead turn to suicide.

Why This Language Is Not Always Taken as Seriously as It Should Be　　When people with depression talk about wanting to *"give up,"* rather than treating this as a warning sign that they could be feeling suicidal, the people around them might instead

- Not realize that their loved one with depression *"giving up"* in this context could equate to them attempting suicide
- Not take what their loved one with depression is telling them as seriously as they otherwise would because they think they are *"just being weak,"* and that rather than *"giving up,"* they *"just need to toughen up"*
- Not take what their loved one with depression is telling them as seriously as they otherwise would because they do not think it is *"rational"* or *"factually correct."* In particular, this may be, for example
  - Because they believe that contrary to what their loved one with depression might be telling them, there are many steps they have *not* yet taken to heal from their depression, and that if they take these steps, they will be able to do so
  - Because they believe that the pain their loved one with depression is in is only temporary, and that because they will get through the difficult times they are going through, there is no sense in them *"giving up"* now
  - Because they believe that their loved one with depression has a *"good life"* that is *"worth living"* – or, at the very least, that their life is not *"bad enough"* for them to *"give up"* on it

Why This Language Should Always Be Taken Seriously   As we hope we have made very clear throughout this book, depression is an extremely painful, challenging, life-altering illness to live with, and one that can convince people that no matter what they do, they will never, *ever* be able to free themselves from it. And, when this is the case, a person with depression who thinks *"I want to give up"* is *not* weak. Rather, this is a very understandable thought when that person is suffering so severely, particularly when they believe that they always will. Consequently, dismissing someone with depression saying *"I want to give up"* by telling them they are *"just being weak"* and that they *"just need to toughen up"* is almost certainly something they will find extremely hurtful. And, because a person with depression saying *"I want to give up"* is a sign that they could be feeling suicidal, dismissing them in this way is also extremely dangerous.

Alternatively, if the people surrounding someone with depression believe that there are still steps that person could take to get better that they have not yet taken, that it is possible for them to make it through the extremely difficult times they are currently going through, and that they have a life that is indeed *"worth living,"* then they are almost certainly correct (to be clear, at The Depression Project, we believe that all lives are *"worth living";* that there are many, many, *many* different steps that can be taken to get better; and that if people with depression continue taking these steps, that in time, it is indeed possible for them to overcome this illness). In saying that, however, it is extremely important to note that people will act based *not* on what is *actually* true, but based on what they *think* is true. Consequently, if a person with depression says they want to *"give up"* because they believe they will never get better and that their life is no longer worth living, then even if the people around them completely disagree with this, the fact that *that person with depression* believes this is a sign that they could be at risk of attempting suicide. And, as a result, if someone with depression talks about wanting to *"give up,"* it should always be taken extremely seriously rather than being dismissed.

Talking Hopelessly About the Future

When a person's depression is so severe that they are talking hopelessly about the future, then it is a notable indicator that they might be feeling suicidal – because the darker their future looks to them, the more they might, to quote one of The Depression Project's community members, *"prefer the nothingness of death."* In particular, some commonly spoken phrases that indicate that someone with depression feels hopeless about their future include the following:

- *"I can't see myself ever getting better."*
- *"Depression has beaten me."*
- *"I feel trapped in my depression and can't see a way out."*
- *"I have no future."*
- *"There is no hope for me."*
- *"Nothing good will ever happen to me again."*
- *"I will never recover from this"* (where *"this"* could mean, for example, depression, a heart-breaking end to a significant relationship, an extremely costly and regrettable mistake they made, or a traumatic, tragic event that took place).
- *"I'll never be happy again."*
- *"I can't see a reason to keep on living."*

Why This Language Is Not Always Taken as Seriously as It Should Be   When people with depression talk hopelessly about the future, rather than treating it as a warning sign that they could be feeling suicidal, the people around them might instead do the following:

- Not recognize the link between someone having no hope for their future and them feeling suicidal.
- Not take what their loved one with depression is telling them as seriously as they otherwise would, because they think they are, for example, *"just being negative," "just being overdramatic," "not thinking rationally,"* and/or *"not factually correct in what they are saying."* In particular, this might be because, for example,

- They believe it is possible for their loved one with depression to get through the difficult, challenging time they are currently going through.
- In their eyes, there are clear reasons why their loved one with depression has a good future ahead of them.

Why This Language Should Always Be Taken Seriously   If the people surrounding someone with depression believe that talking hopelessly about the future is the product of their negative thoughts, and that it is possible for them to make it through the difficult, challenging time they are going through and experience the worthwhile future that they can envision for them, then once again, they are almost certainly correct – particularly because, as we have mentioned,

- Negative thoughts and feelings of hopelessness are very common components of depression.
- Because negative thoughts and feelings of hopelessness are very common components of depression, as we often hear from members of The Depression Project's community, it is *extremely* common for people with depression to view their future much more pessimistically than they otherwise would.

However, once again, people will act based *not* on what is *actually* true, but on what they *think* is true. And, for this reason, if someone with depression believes there is no chance at all of them having the bright future they want, then regardless of how *"factually incorrect"* their loved ones might think this belief is, it is a clear sign that they might be feeling suicidal, and it needs to be taken seriously.

Saying "I'm Such a Burden . . . Everyone Would Be Better Off Without Me"

As we have mentioned multiple times throughout this book, it is common for people with depression to think that they are a *"burden."* And, if they think this negative thought so strongly that they genuinely believe that their friends and family members would be better off if they were no longer alive to *"burden them"* with their depression, then it might lead to them also thinking, *"Me ending my life through suicide would be good for my loved ones, so this is the right thing for me to do."*

Why This Language Is Not Always Taken as Seriously as It Should Be   When people with depression say *"I'm such a burden . . . everybody would be better off without me,"* rather than treating this as a warning sign that they could be feeling suicidal, the people around them might instead do the following:

- Not recognize the link between this language and them actually attempting suicide because they genuinely, wholeheartedly believe that ending their life is the best thing they could possibly do for their loved ones.
- Not take what their loved one with depression is telling them as seriously as they otherwise would because they do not think it is *"rational"* or *"factually correct"* at all. In particular, this is often because they do not view their loved one with depression as being the *"burden"* that they view themselves as being, and/ or because they certainly do *not* agree that *"everybody would be better off without them."*

Why This Language Should Always Be Taken Seriously   Once again, although loved ones of someone with depression might completely disagree that that person is a *"burden"* and that *"everybody would be better off without them"* – and although they might even think that these thoughts are, for example, *"crazy"* – the fact that *that person with depression* believes them means that they could indeed be considering suicide.

Saying **"I Can't Take It Anymore"** */* **"I Can't Go on Like This"** */ Anything Else That Shows That They Are Desperate to Be Free of Their Depression*

In the context of talking about making a *positive change for the better,* having someone with depression say *"I can't take my depression anymore," "I can't go on like this,"* or some variation thereof can be a good sign. For example, if they say,

- *"I'm really going to commit to therapy, because I can't keep going the way I've been going."*
- *"I'm really going to start prioritizing my recovery, because my depression's only been getting worse, and I can't keep going like this."*
- *"As scary as it is for me to do, I know that it's time to reach out for help — because my depression has been getting worse and worse and I just can't take it anymore."*

However, when someone with depression says *"I can't take it anymore," "I can't go on like this,"* or some variation thereof outside of the context of them trying to make a positive change for the better, then it can mean that they have reached the end of their tether; that they no longer feel capable of fighting their depression; and that, as a result, they might be considering turning to suicide.

Why This Language Is Not Always Taken as Seriously as It Should Be When people with depression use this kind of language, rather than treating it as a warning sign that they could be feeling suicidal, the people around them might instead do the following:

- Not recognize the link between their loved one with depression using this kind of language and them actually attempting suicide
- Not take what their loved one with depression is telling them as seriously as they otherwise would because, for example, they do not believe that their loved one's depression is *"so bad"* that it can no longer be tolerated

Why This Language Should Always Be Taken Seriously Although what somebody with depression is going through might not look *"that bad"* to the people around them, it is extremely important to note the following:

- Depression's symptoms are often invisible, and for this reason, what somebody with depression is actually going through is often *significantly* more painful, debilitating, and life-affecting than it might appear to be on the outside.

■ *"How bad"* what a person with depression is going through in the eyes of the people around them is not a determining factor in whether or not that person will actually attempt suicide. Rather, what *is* relevant is that what they are going through feels *"bad enough"* to *"them"* to the point where *they "cannot take it anymore"* / *"cannot go on like this."* And, because this is how they feel – whether justifiably or unjustifiably in the eyes of the people around them – that person using this language is a sign that they could be feeling suicidal.

Talking About Wanting to Escape / Be Free of / No Longer Have Anything to Do with the World

Any comment along these lines is yet another sign that someone with depression might be feeling suicidal. In practice, these comments could take the form of them saying, for example:

■ *"I just want to vanish / disappear."*
■ *"I no longer want to be a part of this world."*
■ *"I wish I could sleep forever and never wake up."*

Furthermore, if this rhetoric is accompanied by that person with depression engaging in reckless behavior that shows a disregard for their own life – such as deliberately crossing a busy street without looking or deliberately driving dangerously – then it is a particularly strong indication that they are feeling suicidal.

Why This Language Is Not Always Taken as Seriously as It Should Be   When people with depression talk about wanting to *"escape,"* *"be free of,"* or *"no longer have anything to do with the world,"* rather than treating this as a warning sign that they might be feeling suicidal, the people around them might instead dismiss it because, for example, they misinterpret it as them *"just looking for attention"* or *"just being overdramatic."*

Why This Language Should Always Be Taken Seriously   Tragically, there are many cases of people dismissing suicide's warning signs as that person *"just looking for attention"* or *"just being overdramatic"* – only for that person to then attempt suicide and end their life. Consequently, to prevent this from happening, we emphatically discourage any warning sign of suicide from being dismissed in this way, and implore loved ones of people with depression to take them seriously instead.

Talking About How Much They Hate Their Life

If someone with depression talks about hating their life, they might be liable to try to end it through suicide.

Why This Language Is Not Always Taken as Seriously as It Should Be   When people with depression talk about *"hating their life,"* rather than treating it as a warning sign that they could be feeling suicidal, the people around them might instead:

- Not recognize the link between them hating their life and them actually attempting suicide.
- Not take what their loved one with depression is telling them as seriously as they otherwise would, because they think they are, for example, *"just being negative," "just being overdramatic,"* and/or *"not thinking rationally."* In particular, this might be because, for example, they believe that their loved one with depression actually has a *"good life"* – or at the very least, a life that is not so bad that it warrants being *"hated."*

Why This Language Should Always Be Taken Seriously   Just because somebody with depression seems to have a *"good life"* according to the people around them – or at the very least, a life that is not so bad that it warrants being *"hated"* – it does *not* mean that that person with depression does not *"hate"* it themselves. After all, although from the *outside* it might appear as if they have a *"good life"* / a life that does not warrant being *"hated,"* on the *inside,* they might be living with, for example, uncontrollable negative thoughts, crippling feelings of worthlessness, a significantly decreased ability to function that is making them furious with themselves, deep feelings of loneliness due to being misunderstood by the people around them, an inability to be able to envision a happy future for themselves, and many other debilitating, painful symptoms of depression that might not be visible on the surface. And, if this is the case – like it is for so many people with depression – then that person might indeed hate their life.

Furthermore, regardless of whether their loved ones believe that their life warrants being *"hated"* or not, what matters is that *that person with depression* hates their life. And, if someone with depression does hate their life – whether justifiably or unjustifiably in the eyes of the people around them – then it is a sign that they might be at risk of attempting suicide.

Saying "I Don't Deserve to Live"

If someone with depression believes that they *"don't deserve to live,"* then there is a risk that they might end their life by suicide, because in their mind, no longer being alive is what they genuinely believe they deserve.

Why This Language Is Not Always Taken as Seriously as It Should Be   When people with depression use this language, then rather than treating this as a warning sign that they might be feeling suicidal, the people around them might instead dismiss it because, for example, they misinterpret it as them *"just looking for attention," "just being overdramatic," "not thinking rationally,"* and/or *"not factually correct in what they are saying."*

Why This Language Should Always Be Taken Seriously
Unfortunately, there are a multitude of reasons why a person with depression might genuinely believe that they *"don't deserve to live."* In particular, some common ones include the following:

- As we have mentioned throughout this book, feeling worthless is a very common component of depression – and, when someone is deep in a depressive episode, it is possible for them to feel so worthless and to hate themselves so much that they wholeheartedly believe *"I don't deserve to live."*

- As we have also mentioned, it is common for people with depression to believe that they are a *"burden"* to the people around them – and, if someone believes this thought with extreme conviction and hates themselves as a result, then it can cause them to also genuinely believe *"I don't deserve to live."*

- As we have also mentioned, it is extremely common for people with depression to feel deeply ashamed of the consequences that can stem from depression's intense, debilitating symptoms – including, for example, being unable (or at least finding it extremely difficult) to function, not being the person they want to be in their relationships, engaging in self-sabotaging behaviors they later regret, and feeling so at the end of their tether that they uncontrollably lash out at their loved ones when they do not deserve it. And, if someone with depression feels extremely ashamed of themselves for one or more of depression's consequences such as these, then it can also cause them to really believe *"I don't deserve to live."*

- If someone has made a very costly and regrettable mistake that they cannot forgive themselves for, then they might feel so consumed with guilt, shame, and self-loathing that they truly believe *"I don't deserve to live."*

Consequently, because people with depression can genuinely, wholeheartedly believe that they *"don't deserve to live"* – and are at risk of attempting suicide as a result – this language needs to be taken extremely seriously.

Speculating About Death

If someone with depression is openly speculating about death, then it could also be a sign they are considering suicide. In practice, this could take the form of them saying, for example,

- *"What do you think happens after we die?"*

- *"If someone suffered throughout their life, then do you think they will be at peace when they're dead?"*
- *"I wonder what it feels like to be dead."*

Why This Language Is Not Always Taken as Seriously as It Should Be Unfortunately, not everyone may see a connection between somebody talking about death in a speculative, philosophical way such as this and that person actually contemplating ending their own life.

Why This Language Should Always Be Taken Seriously If somebody with depression is openly speculating about death, then it is evidence to suggest that death is very much on their mind. And, if this is the case, then it is a strong indication that they might be contemplating suicide.

Talking About Wanting to Die

If someone with depression is talking about wanting to die and/or wanting to be dead, then it is another clear sign that they might be feeling suicidal.

Why This Language Is Not Always Taken as Seriously as It Should Be When people with depression talk about wanting to die and/or be dead, rather than treating it as a warning sign that they could be feeling suicidal, the people around them might instead not take what they are saying seriously at all. In practice, this is often because

- They believe their loved one with depression is *"just looking for attention."*
- Their loved one with depression might be talking about wanting to die and/or be dead in a way that comes off as if they are *"only joking"* – which makes the people around them mistakenly conclude that their loved one with depression is not actually suicidal.

Why This Language Should Always Be Taken Seriously As we have already talked about, dismissing a warning sign of suicide by assuming that that person with depression is *"just looking for attention"* is extremely, extremely dangerous, and something that we strongly advocate against.

Additionally, even if somebody is only talking about wanting to die and/or be dead in a lighthearted, joking way that comes across rather humorously, it is still a sign that they could be feeling suicidal.[2] In particular, as we have heard from members of The Depression Project's community, some common reasons why this is the case include the following:

- If a person's symptoms of depression are so intense that they are feeling suicidal, then they might use humor to try to make what they are going through a little bit lighter.
- If a person's depression has been so long lasting that they are contemplating suicide as a way to finally be free of it, then they might have become desensitized to this "dark" subject matter, and therefore feel much more comfortable making "dark jokes" than somebody who does not have depression and who has no experience of feeling suicidal.
- If a person with depression is feeling suicidal, then joking about wanting to die and/or be dead could be their attempt to broach the topic of suicide in a somewhat indirect, lighthearted way that might feel a bit more comfortable for them than more direct, "serious" ways of opening up about what they are going through.

Consequently, even if it appears as if somebody with depression is *"only joking"* about *"wanting to die"* and/or *"wanting to be dead,"* this language still deserves to be taken very seriously.

Making Comments That Sound as if They Are "Leaving," and That Are Often Associated with "Saying Goodbye"

For example:

- *"I've really enjoyed your friendship. Thanks for everything."*

- *"I hope you always know that no matter what happens, you've been a good sister to me."*
- *"I'm grateful to have had you be a part of my life."*
- *"In case I don't see you again, I love you."*
- *"If I don't get to see you again, then I just want to say goodbye."*

Additionally, if this language is accompanied by that person with depression suddenly and unexpectedly making preparations that are in alignment with the expectation that they will pass away soon – such as them putting together a will and/or giving away their important possessions – then it is a particularly strong sign that they are planning to attempt suicide.

Why This Language Is Not Always Taken as Seriously as It Should Be   Unfortunately, not everyone might see a connection between this language and the person who is speaking to them actually contemplating suicide – and perhaps already planning to take their own life.

Why This Language Should Always Be Taken Seriously   Comments like *"I've really enjoyed our friendship," "you've been a good sister to me,"* and *"I'm grateful to have had you be a part of my life"* could, on the one hand, be coming purely from a place of gratitude, and simply be nothing more than someone showing appreciation for a person they care about. However, when somebody with depression uses language that sounds as if they are *"leaving"* or *"saying goodbye"* – particularly when they do so unexpectedly and abruptly as we have said – then it could also be a sign that they are saying their *"final farewells"* before attempting to end their life. Consequently, to better understand what a person with depression is actually thinking when they use this language, it can help for the person they are talking to to ask them, for example:

- *"Is there any particular reason why you're saying this to me today of all days?"*
- *"It kind of sounds like you are saying 'goodbye.' Is everything OK?"*

■ *"I apologize in advance if you find this question confronting, but I really care about you and I'm worried about you, so I have to ask: it sounds to me as if you are telling me 'goodbye,' and because I know you've been fighting depression, I'm scared that this is because you're thinking about suicide. Please tell me: is there any truth to this?"*

Going from Feeling Extremely Depressed to Talking / Acting in a Way That Comes Across as Very Calm and at Peace

If someone has been in a deep depressive episode and then is talking and/or acting in a way that comes across as if they are now very calm and at peace, then, on the one hand, it of course can be a positive sign – because it might indicate that they have made it through their depressive episode and are now feeling much better. However, on the other hand, particularly if this change takes place suddenly and unexpectedly, it can also be a sign of that person planning to die by suicide, and consequently feeling calm and at peace because they believe that their suffering is going to end soon.

Why This Language and Behavior Is Not Always Taken as Seriously as It Should Be   If someone with depression goes from feeling extremely depressed to talking and/or acting in a way that comes across as very calm and at peace, then it is common for the people around them to only interpret this in a positive way – without being aware of the possibility that unfortunately, it might actually be a sign that their loved one with depression is planning to end their pain through suicide.

Why This Language and Behavior Should Always Be Taken Seriously   Because there is a chance that it might be indicative of someone with depression having made up their mind to take their own life, this language and behavior needs to be taken extremely seriously. In particular, to help determine whether a person with depression is now calm and at peace because they have made it through their depressive episode and therefore feel much better, or because they are still extremely deep in their depressive episode and have made plans to end their own life, a few questions their loved ones could ask them include the following:

- *"I've noticed that you seem much more calm and at peace this week. What would you say has contributed to you feeling this way?"*
- *"You seem to be out of your depressive episode now, would that be fair to say? If so, were there any particular steps that you took to help pull you out of it?"*
- *"Are there any realizations you've had in your healing journey that have encouraged this big change in you?"*
- *"I don't mean to put you on the spot with this question, but I really care about you and I'm worried about you, so I have to ask: I've been trying to learn more and more about depression to help support you better, and I read in a book recently that sometimes the reason people can go from being deep in a depressive episode to appearing very calm like you do now is because they are planning to take their own life, and feel at peace thinking that their pain is about to end. Please tell me: is this the case for you at all?"*

Unexpectedly Talking About / Actively Pursuing Ticking Items Off Their Bucket List

If someone has been in a deep depressive episode and is now unexpectedly talking about and/or actively pursuing ticking items off their bucket list, then just like when it comes to them appearing calm and at peace, on the one hand, it can indeed be a positive sign. In particular, this is because it might indicate that they are now out of their depressive episode, and that because they now have, for example, much more energy, much more motivation, and the ability to be able to experience joy and pleasure again, they want to capitalize on it by pursuing the things that matter the most to them. However, it can also mean that they are intending to end their own life, and are just ticking the things they have always wanted to do off their bucket list before they die.

Why This Language and Behavior Is Not Always Taken as Seriously as It Should Be   If someone with depression unexpectedly goes from feeling extremely depressed to talking about and/

or actively pursuing ticking items off their bucket list, then it is common for the people around them to automatically interpret this as a positive sign – without considering that it might actually be a sign that their loved one with depression is planning to end their own life after they have ticked everything they can off their bucket list.

Why This Language and Behavior Should Always Be Taken Seriously   Because there is a chance that unexpectedly talking about and/or actively pursuing ticking items off their bucket list might be indicative of someone with depression having made up their mind to take their own life, this language and behavior needs to be taken extremely seriously. In particular, to help determine whether a person with depression is taking these steps because they have made it through their depressive episode and are therefore in a much better position to do so, or because they are still trapped in their depressive episode and have made plans to end their own life, a few questions their loved ones could ask them include the following:

- *"I see you're now focusing a lot more on your bucket list of activities that you've always wanted to do. What has sparked this?"*
- *"Is there any breakthrough you've had with your depression that has inspired you to now want to focus on fulfilling the items on your bucket list?"*
- *"Is experiencing the things you've always wanted to experience helping you to have more hope and excitement for the future? Is it whetting your appetite to want to experience more and more?"*
- *"I don't mean to make you feel uncomfortable with this question, but I really care about you and I'm worried about you, so I have to ask: I've been trying to learn more and more about depression to help support you better, and I recently read that sometimes people with depression might quite suddenly focus on ticking items off their bucket list because they are actually intending to end their own life, and they want to experience the things they've always wanted to experience before they do so. Once again, I don't want to make you uncomfortable, but is this the reason why you've started focusing on your bucket list?"*

Some Advice for Supporters if They Pick Up on Their Loved One with Depression Using Language That Signals That They Might Be Feeling Suicidal

In the first part of this chapter, we highlighted the language that people with depression often use that warns they could be feeling suicidal, and emphasized the need for their loved ones to always take this language seriously instead of dismissing it. And, in this second part of the chapter, we are now going to share some additional advice for supporters about what they can do if they pick up on their loved one with depression using language that signals that they might be feeling suicidal in order to help them

1. Remain safe
2. Receive the appropriate level of care and support they need moving forward

With that being said, we will begin by talking about the importance of providing people with depression who are feeling suicidal with a *safe, judgment-free space to talk.*

Give Your Loved One with Depression a Safe, Judgment-Free Space to Talk About What They Are Going Through

When a loved one is deep in a depressive episode to the point when they are using language that indicates that they might be suicidal, then allowing them to talk openly about their feelings without fear of being judged is a wonderful way of supporting them. This is because:

- Talking about their feelings can serve as a cathartic release for your loved one with depression and therefore help them feel a little bit better.
- Having you to talk to can give them comfort in knowing that rather than being all alone in their struggle, they have someone who cares about them and is there to help.

■ Moving forward, knowing they can talk to you safely without the fear of being judged is likely to make them feel more comfortable opening up to you in the future as opposed to suffering in silence all by themselves. And, the more they open up and the less they suffer in silence moving forward, the better they are likely to feel, and as a result, the less likely they also are to feel suicidal.

Try to Better Understand Your Loved One with Depression

The more you understand what your loved one with depression is thinking and feeling, the better placed you will be to help them. On that note, here are some questions that, depending on the circumstances, you might find insightful to ask:

■ *"What are the thoughts that you're thinking right now?"*

■ *"What is causing you to think these thoughts? Are there one or more triggers that you can identify?"*

■ *"What do you feel right now?"*

■ *"What is causing you to feel this way? Are there one or more triggers that you can identify?"*

■ *"How do you feel about the future?"*

■ *"Do you feel like there are things in the future you have to look forward to?"*

■ *"Do you have hope that you can get better?"*

■ *"Why do you feel as if the future is hopeless?"* (if they say they have no hope for the future)

■ *"Do you feel like you know the next steps to get better?"*

■ *"Do you feel like you have a reason to keep on living?"*

■ *"Do you feel like you still have a purpose in life?"*

■ *"Do you ever think that life isn't worth living anymore?"*

■ *"Have you done anything reckless or dangerous or put yourself in harm's way at all, without caring about whether you lived or died? Have you done anything like this with the hope that you would die?"*

■ *"Do you have a plan for how you would attempt suicide that you are thinking about acting on or that you have already decided to act on?"*

- *"Are you contemplating doing something to try to end your life now – even if you aren't sure what that 'something' is? Or, would you say that your suicidal thoughts are thoughts that you have no intention of acting on?"*

Try to Understand Whether Thoughts of Suicide Are Passive or Active for Your Loved One with Depression

There is a critical difference between thoughts of suicide that are *passive* and thoughts of suicide that are *active*. In particular:

- Thoughts of suicide can be considered *passive* when a person with depression might think about suicide and/or fantasize about death, but they currently have no plans or intention to actually end their own life.
- However, thoughts of suicide can be considered *active* when not only does that person with depression think about suicide and/or fantasize about death, but also
  - They have a plan for how to end their life that they are contemplating acting on or have already decided to act on.
  - Or, if they do not have a specific plan in place for how to end their life, they are still actively contemplating doing *something that is yet to be determined* to end their life.

To help determine whether a loved one with depression's suicidal thoughts are *passive* or *active,* questions that can be very helpful to ask them include the following:

- *"Do you have a plan for how you would attempt suicide that you are thinking about acting on or that you have already decided to act on?"* As we have said, if they have a plan for how they would actually attempt suicide that they are contemplating acting on or have already decided to act on, then their thoughts of suicide can be considered *active*.
- *"Are you contemplating doing something to try to end your life now, even if you aren't sure what that 'something' is? Or, would you say*

that you have no intention of acting on your suicidal thoughts?" As we have also said, even if your loved one with depression does *not* have a plan in place for how to attempt suicide, if they are contemplating doing *something that is yet to be determined* to end their life, then their thoughts of suicide can still be considered *active*. However, if they have no intention of acting on their suicidal thoughts, then their thoughts of suicide can be considered *passive* for now.

What to Do if Your Loved One with Depression's Suicidal Thoughts Are Passive

As we have said, your loved one with depression's suicidal thoughts can be considered *passive* when they currently have no plans or intention to end their life. When this is the case, we believe that the following suggestions are helpful ways of supporting them.

Encourage Them to Get Professional Help as Soon as Possible When someone with depression has no plans or intention to end their life – and they are therefore not in imminent risk of danger – we do *not* recommend the following:

- Pressuring them into, for example, immediately calling a suicide hotline or immediately going to the emergency room of their local hospital or a psychiatric institution
- Taking it upon yourself to involve your local emergency services

This is because

- Doing so in this case is likely to leave your loved one with depression feeling frustrated and uncomfortable (if they are being pressured into calling a suicide hotline, going to their local emergency room, or checking into a psychiatric institution, for example, when they are not in imminent risk of danger); and in addition to making them feel frustrated and uncomfortable, it might also make them feel traumatized (in the case of, for example, police arriving at their home to have them committed to a psychiatric institution against their will when they are not in imminent risk of danger).

- As a result of being frustrated, put in an uncomfortable situation, and/or being traumatized, they will likely be much less inclined to open up to you the next time they are having thoughts of suicide.

In saying that, however, we certainly recommend that you strongly encourage your loved one with depression to get professional help as soon as they possibly can. In practice, this could take the form of them, for example, having a consultation with a doctor or a therapist, who can then work with them on developing a plan to keep them safe and help them get better.

Remind Them of All the Reasons They Have to Stay Alive

Additionally, it can also be helpful to remind your loved one with depression of all the reasons they have to stay alive. This is because when someone is so deep in a depressive episode that they are having thoughts of suicide, it is very common for them to have lost touch of these reasons, and being reminded of them can help them see that despite their pain, life is still worth living.

On that note, some of the reasons that your loved one with depression might have to stay alive that you might want to remind them of could include the following:

- All the future life milestones they have to look forward to – such as getting married, having a baby, having grandchildren, going on holidays to their dream destination, and so on
- Their dreams and other goals that they have always wanted to accomplish in life
- Their hobbies and the other things that bring them joy
- Their friends and family who love them

In saying this, however, it is possible that even when you remind your loved one with depression of these reasons they have to stay alive, they will be too consumed by their depression to be able to connect with them. For example:

- They might feel so devoid of hope for the future that they do not think they will get to experience any of the future milestones they would like to experience, or achieve any of the goals or dreams they have for themselves.
- They might feel too numb to be able to enjoy any of their hobbies, and be unable to envision this numbness ever lifting so that they can enjoy them in the future.
- They might think that they are a *"burden"* to their friends and family and that all their loved ones would be better off without them.

And, if this is the case, then it can also be extremely worthwhile for you to do your best to help them *reconnect* with these reasons to stay alive – by highlighting why what they are currently telling themselves about them might not be true. For example:

- If they have lost hope that they will experience the future milestones they want to experience and/or achieve any of their goals and dreams, it can help to
  - Remind them that the reason they are unable to envision these positive events taking place for themselves is *not* because they are unattainable; it is because right now, their depression is clouding their ability to be able to see them happening. And, once this depressive episode has passed, then their future will look significantly brighter, and it will be much easier for them to see that it will indeed be possible for them to experience the milestones they want to experience and to achieve the goals and dreams that they want to achieve.
  - Additionally, it can also help to remind them of their past achievements and any occasions when they have managed to succeed at something after previously doubting they would. This can also help give them hope that they will be able to accomplish their goals and live their dreams moving forward even though right now, doing so seems out of reach.

- If they feel too numb to be able to enjoy any of their hobbies and the other things that they usually would, then it can help to remind them that this numbness is only temporary, and that once they have made it through this depressive episode, they will be able to find pleasure in these activities again.
- If they think that they are a *"burden"* to their loved ones and that they would be *"better off without them,"* then it can help to
  - Remind them of all of the good things they *have brought, do bring,* and *will bring* to their relationships.
  - Remind them of all the positive characteristics they have.
  - Remind them that the reason they think they are a *"burden"* is *not* because they are, but rather, because as we talked about in Chapter 2, they are engaging in distorted thinking patterns that are falsely convincing them that they are a *"burden."*
  - Emphasize that their friends and family who love them would absolutely *not* be better off without them, and that, in reality, they would be absolutely devastated if that person ended their life and was no longer with them.

Try Your Best to Reassure, Encourage, and Empower Your Loved One with Depression   When your loved one with depression is feeling so depressed that they are having thoughts of suicide, then another helpful, effective way of supporting them is to

- Reassure them that the lies their depression is telling them are not true.
- Encourage them to keep on going.
- Empower them to feel better about themselves in spite of all the awful things their depression is telling them.

In particular, some effective ways you can do this include the following:

- Reassure them that they are not alone, because you and everyone else who loves them will always be there to support them.

- Reassure them that they are not the awful things their mind is telling them they are.
- Remind them that they are loved by so many people, even if, because of their depression, they cannot see this right now.
- Remind them that although what they are going through now is extremely difficult, just like they have survived every other difficult experience they have been through in the past, they are going to survive this one, too.
- Reassure them that this too shall pass.
- Reassure them that even if they cannot see any reasons to keep on fighting, it does not mean that there are not any; rather, it just means that their depression is telling them even more lies than usual right now.
- Reassure them that they are not always destined to feel this way, and that with help, they can get better and have the future they want.
- Remind them that no one is too broken, too scarred, or too far gone to beat their depression.
- Reassure them that even though they are struggling with depression, they are still the same amazing person they have always been.
- Reassure them that they are not a burden.
- Remind them of all the good things they have done in their life.
- Reassure them that they are strong and courageous for continuing to fight a debilitating illness that no one can see.
- Tell them how their refusal to give up is inspiring.
- Reassure them that they should feel proud of themselves for everything they have overcome so far.
- Remind them that they are so much more than just their depression.
- Tell them that you believe in them.
- Reassure them that they are stronger than their depression.
- Remind them that you will always love them, even on their darkest days.

Reassuring, encouraging, and empowering your loved one like this is a really great way of helping them combat the lies their depression is telling them, as well as helping them feel more safe, comfortable, and soothed when they are so deep in a depressive episode that they are having thoughts of suicide.

Show Your Support Through Caring, Nonverbal Gestures   In addition to strongly encouraging your loved one with depression to seek professional help as soon as possible, reminding them of the reasons they have to stay alive, reassuring them that the lies their depression is telling them are not true, encouraging them to keep on going, and empowering them to feel better about themselves, your loved one with depression will also likely appreciate being supported through *caring, nonverbal* gestures as well. For example, you could perhaps

- Comfort them by holding their hand and/or hugging them.
- Wrap them up in a cozy warm blanket.
- Run a warm, soothing bath for them to rest and relax in.
- Cook them their favorite food.
- Try to make their environment a bit more comfortable for them – for example, by putting on their favorite music, lighting a candle, or tidying up a little bit.
- Put on their favorite movie or sport and stay with them to watch it.
- Help them with anything they need to get done that might reduce their overwhelm – for example, by doing their grocery shopping, cleaning the dishes, and/or running an errand for them.

What to Do if Your Loved One with Depression's Suicidal Thoughts Are Active

As we have said, your loved one with depression's suicidal thoughts can be considered *active* when

- They have a plan for how to end their life that they are contemplating acting on or have already decided to act on.

■ Or, if they do not have a specific plan in place for how to end their life, they are actively contemplating doing *something that is yet to be determined* to end their life.

When a loved one with depression's thoughts of suicide are *active*, then

■ This is the time for you to strongly encourage them to call a suicide hotline, visit their local emergency ward or psychiatric institution, and/or for your local emergency services to get involved. These services can create a safety plan that is tailored to your loved one to help keep them out of danger, as well as provide direction moving forward for what their next steps should be.

■ You can also help reduce the risk of suicide by creating a safe environment for your loved one by, for example:

    ■ Hiding or removing any weapons, sharp objects, or anything else they could use to attempt suicide.

    ■ Doing out their medication to them yourself to remove the possibility and temptation for them to try to overdose.

    ■ Taking whatever other steps are necessary to prevent your loved one with depression from being able to act on their plan to attempt suicide.

■ We also recommend that you stay with your loved one with depression – because when their thoughts of suicide are *active* in nature, then it can be dangerous to leave them alone.

■ While you stay with them, it can still be helpful to remind them of the reasons they have to stay alive; to try to reassure, encourage, and empower them through the ways we have mentioned; and/or to support them through one or more caring, nonverbal gestures as well.

Next: Depression's "Facial Language Barrier"

In this part of the book, we highlighted the language that people with depression often use that warns that they might be feeling suicidal, and we explained how loved ones of people with depression can help support them, keep them safe, and get the help they need when they are feeling this way. And, in the next part of this book, we are going to work on breaking down the "nonverbal language barriers" that can also exist between people with depression and those around them – starting with depression's *"facial language barrier"* in Chapter 12.

PART III

Depression's "Nonverbal Language Barriers"

12

Depression's "Facial Language Barriers"

In addition to spoken words, facial expressions and interactions are of course also part of the way people communicate. For example:

- Smiling can communicate that a person is happy.
- Scowling can communicate that a person is angry.
- Eye contact can communicate that a person is focused and engaged in a conversation.
- Raised eyebrows can communicate that a person is surprised.

However, in the same way that words and everyday expressions can take on a vastly different meaning than they otherwise would when they are said by someone with depression, so can facial expressions and interactions. And, just like when it comes to depression's "verbal language barrier" that we have thus far focused on throughout this book, this "facial language barrier" can also result in people with depression

- Feeling alone and misunderstood
- Having conflict in their relationships
- Not receiving the support they need
- Consequently feeling even more depressed

For this reason, in this chapter, we are going to identify what the facial expressions and interactions are that can take on a different meaning than they otherwise might when they are coming from someone with depression, as well as share some advice for overcoming this "facial language barrier" moving forward.

What People with Depression Might Actually Be Going Through When They Smile

As we just touched on, smiling is usually thought of as being associated with *positive* emotions – such as happiness, joy, excitement, cheerfulness, and/or peace of mind. However, as we frequently hear from members of The Depression Project's community, it is very, *very* common for people with depression to smile even when they are feeling severely depressed. In particular, according to our community members, some reasons why people with depression might mask it with a smile are as follows:

- *"It's easier than explaining how you really feel."*
- *"I don't want to make the person I'm talking to feel sad or be a burden to them."*
- *"It's more socially acceptable to fake a smile than say how depressed you are."*
- *"When you've opened up to people in the past and they haven't understood, you become conditioned to believe that NO ONE will take your depression seriously. So, regardless of how you actually feel, you just smile and pretend that everything is good."*
- *"I feel like people don't actually care how I really feel, so I just act like everything's fine. There's only a couple of people who I know truly care, so they're the only ones I feel safe enough with to drop the mask."*

Our Advice if You Do Not Have Depression Yourself but You Know Someone Who Does

If someone you know with depression is smiling, although they hopefully are indeed feeling happy and genuinely having a good day, we encourage you not to *automatically assume* that this is the case — particularly if they are in an environment where they might be likely to feel that it would be more "socially acceptable" to blend in and pretend that everything is *"fine"* (such as in a group social setting where everyone is having fun or a work setting where everyone is acting professionally). Instead, we encourage you to do the following:

- Take the time to check in with them and ask how they are — particularly if you *notice one or more signs that their smile might be "fake."* In particular, these signs include
  - That person smiling with their mouth but not their whole face.
  - Their eyes looking sad or devoid of emotion.
  - Their mouth appearing tense rather than relaxed and at ease.
- After asking your loved one with depression how they are, then like we talked about in Chapter 2, it is possible they will respond by saying *"I'm fine"* or *"I'm OK"* even when they are not. And, if this is the case, then we encourage you to follow up by asking them, for example: *"Are you actually OK, or are you just saying that? I'm here to have a proper chat about how you feel if you'd like."*
- In response to this follow-up question, if your loved one with depression repeats that they are *"fine"* or *"OK,"* then, as we also advised in Chapter 2, we encourage you to take a moment to share your willingness to listen to them moving forward if they ever want to talk to you about how they are feeling.
- Last, to help them see that you really care about them — and therefore make them more likely to feel comfortable being open about what they are going through when they are in a depressive episode moving forward — we encourage you to continue checking in on them from time to time as well.

Our Advice if You Have Depression Yourself and Can Relate to Masking It with a Smile

If you have depression yourself and can relate to masking it with a smile, then to help you feel more comfortable being open about what you are actually going through, we would like to remind you of the following suggestions that, in Chapter 2, we shared with you in the context of people with depression hiding how they are feeling by saying *"I'm fine"* or *"I'm OK"* even when they are not.

- If you mask your depression with a smile because you find it easier than being open about how you truly feel, we encourage you to use the Storm to Sun Framework to express what you are going through.

- If you mask your depression with a smile because you think *"I will become a burden if I say how I really feel when I'm in a depressive episode,"* then we encourage you to carefully consider the ways in which this thought could be distorted by *filter thinking, double standards,* and/or *mind reading,* and therefore not an accurate reflection of reality. Additionally, we encourage you to reread the encouraging reminders we shared with you in Chapter 2 that can help you let go of this negative thought, choose one that resonates with you, and then repeat it to yourself anytime you catch yourself thinking that being open about your depression will make you a *"burden."*

What People with Depression Might Actually Be Going Through When They Avoid Making Eye Contact

For multiple reasons, it can be very challenging for people with depression to maintain eye contact during a conversation. However, because these reasons are often not understood by the people they talk to, then

- It can result in those people concluding that that person with depression is not interested in and/or does not care about what they are saying, which can leave them feeling upset, offended, and/or hurt.

- It can result in them concluding that that person with depression is not telling them the truth, which can leave them not trusting that person with depression.
- It can result in them concluding that that person with depression is rude and unfriendly, which might make them not want to interact with them again.

However, the reasons why it can be very challenging for people with depression to maintain eye contact when they are talking to someone is *not* because they are *"disinterested,"* because they *"don't care,"* because they *"aren't telling the truth,"* because they are *"unfriendly,"* or because they are *"rude,"* for example. Rather, according to members of The Depression Project's community, making eye contact can be very challenging because of the following reasons:

- *"If I look someone in the eye when I'm in a depressive episode, I'm scared I'll break down and start crying right then and there. So, I try to avoid people's gaze to help me keep it all together."*
- *"Like many people with depression, I feel worthless, and my self-confidence is very low. It's not easy to look people in the eye when you feel this way about yourself."*
- *"Sometimes, your eyes can give away how you really feel, So, if I'm trying to hide how depressed I am from someone, I'll avoid looking in their eyes so that I don't blow my cover."*
- *"There are times when my depression is just too overpowering for me to fully engage in a conversation. I'll lose track of it sometimes and involuntarily be gazing off into the distance, before being brought back by the person I'm talking to clicking their fingers or loudly saying 'Hey! Hey! Are you listening? Are you listening?' I get that it's frustrating for them, but I swear, I'm not doing it on purpose."*
- *"I have social anxiety as well as depression, so making eye contact with others is twice as difficult for me."*

Our Advice if You Do Not Have Depression Yourself but You Know Someone Who Does Who Often Avoids Making Eye Contact

If someone you know with depression is prone to avoiding making eye contact with you, then

- Rather than holding it against them – such as by concluding that they are *"not telling the truth," "unfriendly,"* and/or *"rude,"* for example – we encourage you to keep in mind that struggling to make eye contact can be yet another impact of the consuming, debilitating illness they are fighting.
- Additionally, please try not to take their lack of eye contact personally – such as by concluding that they *"aren't interested"* and that they *"don't care"* about what you are telling them, or by concluding that because they do not appear to care or be interested in what you are telling them, that what you are telling them therefore must be *"boring."* After all, the reason why they are struggling to make eye contact with you is *not* because of anything that you, personally, are telling them. Once again, it is because of their depression.

Our Advice if You Have Depression Yourself and Find It Very Difficult to Make Eye Contact with Others

If you have depression and find it challenging to make eye contact when you are engaging with other people as a result, then, ideally, the people close to you would understand the reasons why, and as a result, not hold it against you. However, unfortunately many people do *not* understand the reasons why depression can make it so challenging for people to maintain eye contact. If this is the case for the people you interact with, then you may find the following suggestions helpful:

- At some point when you feel up to it, we encourage you to try telling each of these people the reasons *why* you might at times find it challenging to maintain eye contact with them. If you understandably do not feel comfortable doing this face-to-face – when you of course might feel pressured to make eye contact with them – then you will likely find it easier to instead, for example, send them a message that explains these reasons and/or show them this section of this book.

■ Additionally, rather than maintaining eye contact with a person when you are speaking to them, then in some cases at least, you might find it a worthwhile strategy to look *near* the person's eyes rather than directly into them – for example, by looking at their eyebrows, their nose, or their cheeks instead. This strategy can help prevent people from thinking that you are *"disinterested," "don't care," "not telling the truth," "unfriendly,"* and/or *"rude"* for not making eye contact with them, while at the same time being much more within your comfort zone than directly meeting a person's eyes.

What People with Depression Might Actually Be Going Through When Their Facial Expressions Are Muted

When someone is deep in a depressive episode and either choosing not to mask their depression with a smile or is feeling too depressed to be able to do so, then it is common for their facial expressions to be *muted* as a result. Or, to put it another way, it is common for their faces to show very little emotion, and to react very minimally (if at all) whenever someone is speaking to them. And, if the person they are speaking to does not understand the reason why, then

■ It can result in that person concluding that their loved one with depression is not being a good friend / partner / sibling and so on, for example, if in response to some good news they share, their loved one with depression is not showing the level of enthusiasm and excitement they believe is appropriate.

■ As is the case with lack of eye contact, it can result in them concluding that their loved one with depression is not interested in and/or does not care about what they are saying, which can leave them feeling upset, offended, and/or hurt.

However, the reason why it is common for people with depression to have muted facial expressions when they are deep in a depressive episode is *not* because they are, for example, a *"bad friend / partner / sibling"* and so on, or because they are *"disinterested"* and/or *"don't care"* about what someone is saying to them. Rather, it is because, as we have talked about throughout this book, when someone is deep in a depressive episode, they are being weighed down by some or all of the following symptoms:

- Uncontrollable negative thoughts – such as *"I'm a loser," "I'm unlovable," "I'm worthless," "I'm a failure," "I'm a burden," "I'm useless," "I deserve to suffer," "I'm not worthy of anything good happening to me," "everybody else is better and more important than I am," "I have no future," "there's no point in doing anything," "everything I do will be a failure," "I will never feel happy again," "I will never overcome depression," "none of my dreams will ever come true,"* and/or *"there's no point in being alive anymore"*
- Excruciatingly painful emotions – such as misery, worthlessness, shame, guilt, regret, and/or hopelessness
- Debilitating physical symptoms – such as complete and utter exhaustion
- Numbness – in the sense that they feel completely disconnected from the world around them, including from anybody who is speaking to them

And, when this is the case, it is very natural that the facial expressions of people with depression might be much more muted than they would otherwise be. Consequently, if you know someone with depression who is prone to having muted facial expressions when they are in a depressive episode, then we encourage you to try the following:

- Rather than holding it against them, please remind yourself that when your loved one with depression is in a depressive episode, they are deeply suffering – which is the real reason why they, for example, are not appearing as enthusiastic, excited, and/or interested in what you are telling them as they otherwise would.

- Additionally, as we said when we were talking about lack of eye contact, please try not to take their muted facial expressions personally. Once again, the reason why their facial expressions are muted is because of the enormous toll that their depression is taking on them, *not* because of anything to do with you or what you are telling them.

What People with Depression Might Actually Be Going Through When They Look Exhausted

As opposed to their facial expressions being muted, it is also possible that when someone is fighting depression, they will instead look exhausted. In particular:

- Their eyelids might be drooping.
- Their eyes might be absent of any gleam or sparkle.
- Their mouth might be hanging open to a degree.
- They might be yawning frequently.

And, if a person with depression comes across as very tired when they are having a conversation with someone, then as is the case with a lack of eye contact and muted facial expressions, it can result in the person they are talking to thinking that they are *"disinterested in what they're saying," "don't care,"* and/or are *"rude,"* for example. However, as we talked about in detail in Chapter 4, exhaustion is a very common symptom of depression – often because of the following reasons:

- Being weighed down by depression's symptoms every day can leave a person feeling extremely tired.
- Feeling as if they have to constantly pretend they are fine when they are not can leave them feeling extremely tired.
- Taking antidepressant medication can make them feel extremely tired.

- Having night after night of disrupted sleep due to uncontrollable negative thoughts and/or nightmares can leave them feeling extremely tired.
- Continuously giving their all to get better but never feeling as if they make any progress can leave them feeling extremely tired.

And, for these reasons, someone with depression appearing exhausted during a conversation is not something to take personally or to hold against them.

What People with Depression Might Actually Be Going Through When They Look Angry

As we have also touched on, depression can cause people to feel angry. In particular, this is often because of the following reasons:

- It is common for people to feel angry that they have depression, and that they consequently have to endure the negative thoughts, the painful emotions, and all of the other unwanted symptoms this illness can entail.
- It is common for people to feel angry when, as opposed to being in control of their negative thoughts and the painful emotions they are feeling, it feels as if those negative thoughts and painful emotions are instead controlling them.
- It is common for people to feel angry over what we at The Depression Project call the "consequences of depression" – which can include, as we have mentioned before, finding it extremely difficult to function, engaging in self-sabotaging behaviors that they are later mad at themselves for engaging in, noticeable weight gain or weight loss, and/or forgetting things that are important to them, for example.
- It is common for people with depression to suppress their emotions until, as one of our community members put it, they *"explode like a volcano."* In particular, this is often because, for reasons we have already talked about, it is common for people

with depression to hide what they are going through from other people.

- It is common for people with depression to feel angry when their depression is misunderstood and/or dismissed by others.

Sometimes, people with depression might be able to hold in this anger, and prevent it from being noticeable. However, at other times, it might become visible on their face, and if they happen to be around somebody else at that time, then it can cause that person to wonder, for example:

- *"Are they angry at me?"*
- *"Did I do something by mistake to upset them?"*
- *"What have I done wrong?"*

Consequently, to overcome this "facial language barrier" and avoid this misunderstanding:

- If someone you care about with depression appears angry and frustrated in your presence and you are unable to identify an obvious reason why, we encourage you *not* to automatically assume that they are angry and frustrated with *you* – because it could just be a product of their depression. Instead, we encourage you to ask them if you have done anything to upset them. If it turns out that you have, then you can take the necessary steps to resolve the matter with them. However, if it turns out that they are not angry with you and that it is actually their depression that is causing them to feel this way, then you can at least have some peace of mind knowing that everything is OK between the two of you, and then do your best to support your loved one with depression who is clearly going through a lot.
- Alternatively, if you have depression yourself and can relate to at times feeling angry as a result, then we encourage you to try your best to be mindful of the ways in which this anger might come across to others, and the uncertainty that it can create for

them. And, if you catch yourself gritting your teeth, scowling, and/or doing anything else as a result of your depression-related anger in the presence of someone else, then we encourage you to clarify that it is not them that you are angry at. In practice, you could do this by saying something along the lines of *"I'm sorry if I seem really frustrated right now. It's not because of you; it's because [insert depression-related reason]."*

Next: Depression's "Touch Language Barrier"

In this chapter, to overcome the "facial language barrier" between people with depression and those around them, we identified the facial expressions and interactions that can take on a different meaning than they otherwise would when they are coming from someone with depression, as well as explained what people with depression might actually be going through in each of these cases. Next, in Chapter 13, we are going to talk about yet another common nonverbal language barrier between people with depression and those around them: depression's "touch language barrier."

13 | Depression's "Touch Language Barriers"

In addition to creating a "verbal language barrier" and a "facial language barrier," depression can also create a "touch language barrier" – in the sense that when people with depression do not initiate, do not engage in, and/or outright avoid physical contact and intimacy, it can take on an extremely different meaning than it would if someone who does *not* have depression withdrew in this way. Consequently, in this chapter

- We will identify some common ways in which people often shy away from physical contact and intimacy when they are in a depressive episode.
- We will explain the ways in which this physical withdrawal is commonly misunderstood, as well as the relationship conflict that it can lead to.

- We will explain the reasons why depression can cause people to be significantly less tactile and physically intimate than they would otherwise be.
- We will explain the steps that partners of someone with depression can take to overcome this "touch language barrier."
- We will explain the steps that people with depression can take to overcome this "touch language barrier."

As we have just hinted at, depression's "touch language barrier" is most prevalent between people with depression and their romantic partners, and for this reason, this relationship dynamic is the one we will focus on throughout this chapter. However, this "touch language barrier" can still be present to a lesser extent in nonromantic relationships as well, and if this is the case for you, then you will still find most of the suggestions that we share to overcome it relevant.

The Ways in Which People with Depression Are Often Less Tactile and Physically Intimate Than They Would Otherwise Be

Although some people with depression might seek out *more* physical contact than they otherwise would – such as if they like to be comforted in a depressive episode by having their partner hold their hand and cuddle them – as we have said, it is also common for people with depression to be much *less* tactile and physically intimate. In particular, some common examples of this include the following:

- Not hugging their partner, hugging them robotically, and/or quickly pulling away from them after being hugged
- Not initiating physical affection with their partner – including, for example, not reaching out to hold their hand while they are walking somewhere, not rubbing their neck after a hard day at work, not wrapping their arms around them from behind while they are chopping vegetables for dinner, not snuggling up close

to them while they are watching television, and not stroking their skin while they are lying in bed preparing to fall asleep

■ Not being responsive to physical affection when it is initiated by their partner – for example, by appearing "lifeless" when their partner touches them, by tensing their muscles, by directly telling their partner not to touch them, or by moving the part of their body that is being touched by their partner away from them

■ Not initiating a kiss with their partner, seeming dispassionate when being kissed by them, quickly disengaging from kissing them, or avoiding kissing them altogether

■ Not initiating sex with their partner, seeming dispassionate or disinterested during sex, or avoiding it altogether

How Physical Withdrawal Is Often Misinterpreted by Partners of People with Depression

There are a wide variety of natural, understandable reasons why depression can cause someone to be much less tactile and physically intimate than they would otherwise be. However, if, like so many people who have never personally experienced depression before, partners of people with depression are not aware of these reasons, then they are likely to take this physical withdrawal personally. And, if this is the case, then it can result in them, for example:

■ Feeling rejected

■ Feeling confused as to whether or not they might have done something wrong to upset their partner with depression

■ Feeling resentful toward their partner with depression (particularly if they conclude that the reason their partner is not fulfilling their physical needs is because they *"can't be bothered to,"* because they *"don't care enough about them to,"* and/or because they are *"just being lazy"*)

■ Feeling insecure in the relationship (particularly if they conclude that their partner with depression's physical withdrawal is evidence that they might no longer be attracted to them, that they might no longer love them, that they might soon leave them, and/or that they might be cheating on them with somebody else)

■ Feeling less close and connected to their partner with depression.

And, if they feel these emotions, then it can naturally lead to conflict with their partner with depression, and/or to them withdrawing themselves in response. Of course, this will likely then result in their partner with depression feeling alone, unsupported, and even more depressed, which will likely result in their partner with depression withdrawing even more, and so the cycle continues and continues.

The Actual Reasons Why People with Depression Might Be Much Less Tactile and Physically Intimate Than They Would Otherwise Be

However, as opposed their partner with depression being *"upset"* with them, *"lazy,"* no longer *"attracted"* to them, no longer *"in love"* with them, about to *"leave them,"* or *"cheating on them,"* the actual reason why people with depression might withdraw from touch and physical intimacy is because it can be a very natural, very understandable consequence of the debilitating illness they are fighting. In particular, we would now like to explain several common reasons for this.

Depression Can Cause People to Feel Numb, Which Can Blunt Their Responsiveness to Physical Touch and Intimacy and Their Desire to Partake in It

As we have mentioned, depression can cause people to feel numb — often because, among other reasons, people with depression can gradually become desensitized to their suffering, because numbness can be a defense mechanism to protect themselves from unbearably painful emotions, and because numbness is a common side effect of antidepressant medication. And, if a person with depression feels numb, there are two reasons in particular why it can cause them to be significantly less tactile and physically intimate than they would otherwise be:

- As we often hear from members of The Depression Project's community, numbness is associated with feeling emotionless. And, because a person's emotions are a major driver of physical touch and intimacy, being devoid of emotion can cause people with depression to be significantly less likely to feel the urge to, for example, hug their loved ones, kiss their partner, make love to their partner, or initiate any other form of physical contact.
- As we also often hear from members of The Depression Project's community, when someone with depression is feeling numb, their senses can be significantly dulled. Consequently, they are much less likely to be responsive to, enjoy, and be stimulated by physical touch and intimacy than they otherwise would be.

Depression Can Cause People to Feel Absolutely Exhausted, and Lack the Energy to Engage in Physical Intimacy

In addition to feeling numb, exhaustion is another major reason why people with depression might be much less likely to initiate sex – and in many cases, might completely avoid it. Additionally, because "depression tiredness" can make even the simplest, smallest of tasks feel like "too much," even acts of physical intimacy that require limited movement or energy might feel beyond their capacity.

People with Depression Might Think Negative Thoughts That Can Contribute to Them Being Less Tactile and Physically Intimate Than They Would Otherwise Be

In particular, these negative thoughts might include the following:

- *"I'm unlovable," "I'm not good enough for my partner," "I'm not worthy of my partner's love,"* and/or *"I'm such a disappointment to them,"* which are thoughts that can stem from, among other sources, the feelings of worthlessness that often consume people with depression. And, when people with depression think these thoughts, it can cause them to not have enough confidence to initiate physical touch and intimacy themselves, and to also feel uncomfortable receiving and/or partaking in physical touch and intimacy when their partner initiates it.

- *"I've become so ugly and unattractive,"* which is a thought that is common for people with depression to have as a result of, for example, struggling with low self-confidence and feelings of worthlessness, noticeable weight gain due to "comfort eating" as a way of coping with their depression, noticeable weight loss due to their appetite being suppressed as a result of their depression, and/or being too "depression tired" to put as much effort as they would like to into their physical appearance. And, the more *"unattractive"* and *"ugly"* people feel, the less confident and comfortable they will likely be having physical intimacy with their partner.

- *"My partner will leave me soon because I'm such a burden to them,"* which is yet another thought that can cause people with depression to feel less confident and comfortable around their partner, and therefore less confident and comfortable initiating, engaging in, and being receptive to physical intimacy with them.

Depression Can Heighten People's Emotions to the Point Where They Feel Extremely on Edge, and When This Is the Case, They Might Not Want to Be Touched

For example:

- Depression can cause people to feel very angry and frustrated, and when someone is in this state, they might not want to be touched.

- Depression can significantly reduce people's ability to function, and therefore make everything they have to do feel overwhelming for them. And, when people are feeling overwhelmed, stressed out, and on the verge of a breakdown in particular, they might also not feel like being touched by anyone.

Depression Can Cause People to Need More "Alone Time" Than They Would Otherwise Need

In particular, some common reasons for this are because people with depression may want time to, for example:

- Make sense of their thoughts
- Process their complex emotions
- Rest and recharge their batteries
- Think about something their therapist told them
- Read a self-help book written by a therapist to try to help them get better
- Practice self-care to help them cope with their depression

And, the more "alone time" people need, the less time they have to, for example, lie down and cuddle with their partner, watch television holding each other's hands, and engage with them in other ways that involve physical touch and intimacy.

Depression Can Cause Erectile Dysfunction, Reduced Libido, and Reduced Ability to Self-Lubricate

Consequently, particularly when they are in a depressive episode, some people with depression find that they are much less likely to engage in sexual intimacy with their partner than they otherwise would.

How to Navigate This "Touch Language Barrier" if You Are in a Relationship with Someone with Depression

If you are in a relationship with someone with depression, then navigating depression's "touch language barrier" is an important part of ensuring that you feel safe, secure, and satisfied in the relationship. And, with these objectives in mind, we would like to share two suggestions with you.

To Properly Understand the Reasons Why Your Partner with Depression Is Physically Withdrawing from You, Ask Them

As we have said, when someone with depression shies away from physical touch and intimacy, it is common for their partner to jump to conclusions about why this is – such as by thinking

- *"What did I do wrong to upset them?"*
- *"They're so lazy for not putting in more effort to attend to my physical needs."*
- *"Maybe they're not attracted to me anymore."*
- *"They're falling out of love with me."*
- *"Maybe the reason they don't want to have sex with me anymore is because they're having sex with somebody else."*

However, rather than jumping to these worst-case-scenario conclusions, we encourage you to instead *ask* your partner why they have physically withdrawn from you. This is because

- In many cases, the reason why your partner has physically withdrawn from you will *not* be because of anything to do with you personally. Rather, as we have said, it will be due to their depression and the enormous effect it is having on them. And, when this is the case, then as opposed to feeling rejected, confused, resentful, insecure in the relationship and/or disconnected from your partner as a result of jumping to worst-case scenarios, understanding this can help you to feel reassured of your partner's love, attraction, and commitment to you.
- Your partner telling you the ways in which their depression is causing them to be less tactile and physically intimate with you will help you to understand them and their depression better. And, as a result, you will likely feel closer and more connected to them moving forward, in addition to being in a better

position to be able to help and support them through their depression as well.

- If it turns out that your partner has physically withdrawn for a reason that *is* actually to do with you personally, then regardless of whatever it might be, talking about it with them can help you know what steps you can take moving forward to resolve the situation.

Try Your Best to Reassure Your Partner with Depression

As we have talked about, a major reason why someone with depression might physically withdraw is because of all the negative things they are telling themselves. And, if this is the case for your partner with depression, then repeated reassurance can help to counteract this negative self-talk, and consequently make them feel safer and more at ease being tactile and physically intimate with you.

In practice, you could do this by reassuring your loved one, for example:

- They are safe with you.
- You see their worth even if their depression is making it difficult for *them* to be able to see it.
- You appreciate them.
- You feel lucky to be with them.
- You are attracted to them.
- They are not alone in their fight against depression.
- They are not a burden to you.

How to Navigate This "Touch Language Barrier" if You Have Depression

If you have depression yourself and can recognize this "touch language barrier" existing between you and your partner (or anybody else), then to try to overcome it and minimize the misunderstandings that it can cause moving forward, we think you'll find the following suggestions helpful.

Try Your Best to Explain the Reason(s) Why Depression Can Make You Less Tactile and Physically Intimate Than You Would Otherwise Be

Openly communicating this is something we highly recommend, because if your partner understands that it is actually your depression that is causing you to physically withdraw, then they will be much less likely to take this personally.

Reassure Your Partner

Another step you can take to help prevent your partner from taking your physical withdrawal personally and thinking that you are *"no longer attracted to them,"* that you *"no longer love them,"* and/or that you are *"about to leave them,"* for example, can be to reassure them of your love, commitment, and attraction to them. To do this, you could perhaps, for example:

- Compliment them on their appearance.
- Acknowledge the traits you like most in your partner and praise them for these traits.
- Express your appreciation and gratitude for them, the nice things they do for you, and for their patience and understanding as you navigate depression.
- Say *"I love you."*

Try to Be Tactile and Engage in Physical Intimacy in the Ways You Can Manage

For example:

- Although giving your partner a massage might be beyond your capacity when you are "depression tired," an alternative way of physically connecting with them might be to cuddle up in bed together and watch a movie.

■ Although you might prefer not to have sexual intercourse, you might feel open to hugging, kissing, and/or other forms of physical intimacy, for example.

If you and your partner are able to work as a team to be tactile and physically intimate in the ways you can manage, it can contribute to you both feeling closer together, more connected to each other, and more satisfied in your relationship than you otherwise would.

Next: Some Final Words to Help You Overcome Depression's "Language Barrier"

In this chapter, we identified the ways in which people might withdraw from physical touch and intimacy when they are in a depressive episode, clarified the reasons why they might do so, and explained what people with depression and their partner can do to overcome this "touch language barrier" and prevent it from causing conflict in their relationship. And, now that we have covered depression's "verbal language barrier," "facial language barrier," and "touch language barrier" in this book, in the next and final section, we are going to recap some of the key points we've talked about, as well as share some parting advice to help people with depression and those supporting them continue navigating depression's "language barrier" moving forward.

Conclusion

A Brief Recap + One Last Suggestion to Help You Continue Navigating Depression's "Language Barriers" Moving Forward

After 13 chapters, we are now almost at the end of this book, and, as a result, it is our hope that you now

- Have a much deeper understanding of the "language barrier" that exists between people with depression and those around them.
- Feel much more comfortable navigating this "language barrier" moving forward, which can
  - Help prevent misunderstandings and conflict in your relationships.
  - Lead to someone with depression – whether that be you or a loved one you care about – receiving much-needed support for this illness, and feeling significantly better as a result.

However, before we bring this book to a close, we would like to briefly recap some of the key points from each chapter, as well as share one last suggestion to help you effectively navigate depression's "language barrier" moving forward.

A Reminder of Some of the Most Important Takeaways from Each Chapter in This Book

- **Chapter 1: What People with Depression Actually Mean When They Say "*I Have Depression.*"** Depression is much, *much* more than *"just being sad."* This is because depression is longer lasting than sadness; and because in addition to sadness, depression can encompass a wide variety of other symptoms as well, including negative thoughts, feelings of worthlessness, apathy, numbness, extreme exhaustion, difficulty concentrating, short-term memory issues, a drastically diminished ability to function, anger, loneliness, shame, lack of motivation, feelings of hopelessness, body aches and pains, headaches, nausea, loss of appetite, and difficulty having sex (including impotency).
- **Chapter 2: What People with Depression Actually Mean When They Say *"I'm Fine"* or *"I'm OK."*** Just because someone with depression says *"I'm fine"* or *"I'm OK"* does not mean that they actually are. In particular, two common reasons why someone with depression might pretend that they are *"fine"* or *"OK"* even when they are not is because they do not know how to put their depression into words, or because they do not want to be a *"burden"* to their loved ones.
- **Chapter 3: What People with Depression Actually Mean When They Say *"Leave Me Alone."*** There are various reasons why someone with depression might want time to themselves. However, sometimes someone with depression might say *"leave me alone"* even when they want the person they are speaking with to stay with them, because they are scared of being a *"burden."*
- **Chapter 4: What People with Depression Actually Mean When They Say *"I'm Tired."*** "Depression tiredness" is very,

very different to "normal tiredness," and it can be so debilitating that even simple tasks, such as cleaning the dishes, having a shower, or getting out of bed, can feel overwhelming and unmanageable.

- **Chapter 5: What People with Depression Actually Mean When They Say** *"I Can't … ."* When someone with depression says that they *"can't"* do something, it is not because they are *"lazy."* Rather, it is because depression can significantly inhibit a person's ability to function – due to how exhausted it can make them feel; how difficult it can make it for them to be able to concentrate; and how much it can sabotage a person's self-worth and confidence, and therefore convince them that they *"can't."*

- **Chapter 6: What People with Depression Actually Mean When They Say** *"I'm Busy."* When the opportunity to spend time with a loved one arises, someone with depression might say *"I'm busy"* not because, for example, they are *"avoiding"* that person or no longer *"care about"* them. Rather, they might say *"I'm busy"* as an excuse to socially withdraw and be by themselves, which is something they might feel the urge to do in order to deal with the significant impact that their depression is having on them.

- **Chapter 7: What People with Depression Actually Mean When They Say** *"I Want to Go Home."* When someone with depression says *"I want to go home"* earlier than the people they are with would expect them to, it is not because they are *"rude," "selfish,"* or *"boring,"* for example. Rather, it is because of the overwhelming impact their depression is having on them, which is making continuing to "stay out" no longer feel manageable.

- **Chapter 8: What People with Depression Actually Mean When They Say** *"I Don't Care."* When someone with depression says *"I don't care,"* it is not because they are trying to *"upset," "offend,"* or *"hurt"* the person they are talking to, or because they *"do not care about them."* It is because they are currently significantly affected by depression's symptoms, and as a result, they currently lack the capacity to give their input on something, make a decision about something, or feel as much emotion toward something as they otherwise would.

- **Chapter 9: What People with Depression Actually Mean When They Say *"I'm Not Hungry."*** If someone with depression says *"I'm not hungry"* and declines to eat, it does not mean that, for example, they are being *"fussy," "picky," "overdramatic," "attention-seeking," "rude,"* or *"ungrateful,"* or that there is an issue with the person or people they are declining to eat with. Rather, it could mean that they have no appetite at all (which is a symptom of depression); that they feel too nauseous to eat (which is another symptom of depression); that because they are so weighed down by depression's symptoms, organizing a meal for themselves feels too overwhelming; or that they have minimal interest in eating because their depression is making them feel numb, and as a result, their tastebuds are dulled.

- **Chapter 10: What People with Depression Actually Mean When They Say *"I'm Having a Good Day."*** People with depression experience varying intensities of symptoms at different times – as opposed to feeling miserable and suffering from the most extreme form of their symptoms 100% of the time – and for this reason, it is possible for people with depression to have days where they feel *"good."* Consequently, if someone with depression says *"I'm having a good day,"* it does not mean that they were previously *"faking it," "making it up," "looking for attention,"* or *"just being overdramatic"* when they said that they struggled with depression. Additionally, neither does it mean that they have now overcome their depression, and that as a result, if at any point in the future they claim to be feeling depressed, then they must be *"faking it," "making it up," "looking for attention,"* or *"just being overdramatic."*

- **Chapter 11: The Language People with Depression Use That Can Mean They Are Suicidal.** There are many verbal warning signs that indicate that someone with depression could be feeling suicidal – all of which need to be taken very seriously instead of being ignored or dismissed. In particular, these include that person with depression saying *"I want to give up"*; talking hopelessly about the future; saying *"I'm such a burden … everyone would be better off without me"*; saying *"I can't take it anymore"* / *"I can't go on like this"* / anything else that shows that they are desperate to be free of their depression; talking about wanting to escape / be free of / no longer have anything to do with the world; talking about how much they hate their life; saying *"I don't deserve to live"*; speculating about death; talking about wanting to die; making comments that sound as if they are "leaving" / that are often associated with "saying goodbye"; suddenly going from feeling extremely depressed to talking / acting in a way that comes across as very calm and at peace; and unexpectedly talking about / actively pursuing ticking items off their bucket list.

- **Chapter 12: Depression's "Facial Language Barrier."** In the same way that words and everyday expressions can take on a vastly different meaning than they otherwise would when they are said by someone with depression, so too can facial expressions and interactions. This is because people with depression might smile when they feel severely depressed; because it can be difficult for people with depression to make eye contact when they are talking to someone; and because depression can cause people to at times have muted facial expressions, look absolutely exhausted, or look angry and frustrated.

- **Chapter 13: Depression's "Touch Language Barrier."** If someone with depression does not initiate, does not engage in, and/or outright avoids physical contact and intimacy with their partner, then it does not mean that, for example, they are *"upset"* with them, *"lazy,"* no longer *"attracted"* to them, no longer *"in love"* with them, about to *"leave them,"* or are *"cheating on them."* Rather, the actual reason why people with depression might withdraw from touch and physical intimacy is because it can be a very natural, very understandable consequence of all the symptoms they are dealing with.

**One Last Suggestion: Any Time a Problem Arises,
Consider *What Role Could Depression's "Language Barrier"
Be Playing in This?***

As we have looked at in detail throughout this book, there are many
different ways in which depression's "language barrier" can cause
problems between people with depression and their loved ones who
are trying their best to support them. And, for this reason, whether
you are the person with depression or the supporter, any time you
have a problem with the other person, we encourage you to stop and
ask yourself this question:

> *"What role could depression's 'language barrier' be playing in this?"*

Of course, there might be some incidents where you conclude
that depression's "language barrier" is not a factor. However, there are
many situations in which you are likely to conclude that depression's
"language barrier" is indeed the underlying cause – or at least that it
might be the underlying cause – of the problem you are having. And,
when this is the case, it is a very, *very* important observation to make
for two reasons in particular.

The first is that any blame for this problem that you placed on the
other person will be rightfully redirected toward depression's
"language barrier." Consequently, any negative emotions you feel
toward that person due to blaming them for this problem will then
significantly diminish – which is an important step toward resolving
the issue you are having with them.

Second, pinpointing that depression's "language barrier" is actually to blame for this issue can lead to you contemplating a second
very important question that we also encourage you to ask yourself:

> *"What steps could I take to try to overcome depression's 'language barrier'
> in this situation, and therefore hopefully resolve this problem that I'm hav-
> ing with my loved one?"*

For example:

- If you are the person with depression in this situation, then to help your loved one understand you better, could you provide them with more detail about how depression is affecting you right now? Would it be possible for you to explain what you need and/or the way you would like to be supported in this situation with a bit more clarity?
- Alternatively, if you are supporting a loved one with depression in this situation, then to understand them better, could you ask them more questions about how their depression is affecting them right now? Could you seek clarification on why they did or did not do something instead of making assumptions, jumping to conclusions, and/or taking their actions personally?

If you reflect on these steps like so and then take the appropriate course of action, then

1. It can contribute to you resolving this particular problem that you are having with your loved one.
2. Because you will both understand each other better, it is likely to result in less problems moving forward as well.
3. Because you will both understand each other better moving forward, you will have an improved relationship with your loved one. Additionally:
   - If you are the supporter in this context, it will be much easier for you to support your loved one with depression.
   - If you are the person with depression in this context, it will be much easier for you to receive the support you need from your loved one.

We Look Forward to Continue Helping You

Now that we have shared our last suggestion for navigating depression's "language barrier," we have officially reached the end of this book. From the bottom of our hearts, we hope you have found it helpful, and we also hope that – whether you have depression yourself or are supporting someone who does – all the work we do at The Depression Project can continue helping you moving forward as well.

All our love,
The Depression Project Team.
www.thedepressionproject.com

Questionnaire to Help You Identify What the Storm Zone, the Rain Zone, and the Cloud Zone Look Like for You

As we talked about in Chapter 2:

- A common reason why people with depression might say *"I'm fine"* or *"I'm OK"* even when they are not is because when they are in a depressive episode, it can be really difficult to describe what they are going through and put it into words.

- If you can relate, then the Storm to Sun Framework can make it significantly easier for you to quickly put your depression into words, and make it significantly easier for the people around you to instantly understand how you are feeling at any moment in time.

Consequently, in this appendix, you will find a questionnaire that, through a series of check boxes and fill-in-the-blank questions, holds your hand through identifying what the Storm Zone, the Rain Zone, and the Cloud Zone look like for you. Once you have completed it, we encourage you to share it with the people whom you want to understand your depression better – so that they can understand what you are going through in each of these zones. We think this is something you might benefit from, because moving forward, it will mean that rather than struggling to communicate how you are feeling and therefore hiding your depression by saying *"I'm fine"* or *"I'm OK,"* you can instead identify what zone of the Storm to Sun Framework you are currently in – at which point, the person you are talking to will instantly have a snapshot of how you are actually feeling, what your current capacity to function is, and how you would like to be supported at that moment in time.

With that being said, as soon as you are ready, we encourage you to complete the questionnaire that follows.

Part 1: The Storm Zone of the Storm to Sun Framework

When someone is in the Storm Zone of the Storm to Sun Framework, it means that the intensity of their depressive symptoms are severe. To identify what you tend to experience when you are in the Storm Zone, we encourage you to check the boxes that apply to you, and when prompted, fill in the blanks as well.

☐ When I am in the Storm Zone, I am usually battling a lot of negative thoughts.

In particular, these negative thoughts include (circle / underline / highlight the ones that apply): *"I'm a loser."* / *"I'm unlovable."* / *"I'm worthless."* / *"I'm a failure."* / *"I'm a burden."* / *"I'm useless."* / *"I deserve to suffer."* / *"I'm not worthy of anything good happening to me."* / *"Everybody else is better and more important than I am."* / *"Nothing good will ever happen to me."* / *"I have no future."* / *"There's no point in doing anything."* / *"Everything I do will be a failure."* / *"I will never feel happy again."* / *"I will never overcome depression."* / *"None of my dreams will ever come true."* / *"I will never be free of my pain."* / *"Everybody would be better off without me."* / *"There's no point in being alive anymore."*

Additionally, here are other negative thoughts I often think in the Storm Zone:

_____

_____

_____

_____

_____

☐ When I am in the Storm Zone, I usually feel miserable.

☐ When I am in the Storm Zone, I usually do not have much interest in things, including the things that when I am not in the Storm Zone I usually enjoy.

☐ When I am in the Storm Zone, I am usually drained of energy and feel exhausted.

☐ When I am in the Storm Zone, even what would otherwise be relatively simple tasks can feel overwhelming for me.

In particular, these tasks include (circle / underline / highlight the ones that apply): *getting out of bed / showering / doing the dishes / taking the trash out / cooking / exercising / working / interacting with other people / going outside*

Additionally, other things I usually find overwhelming in the Storm Zone include the following:

_____

_____

_____

☐ When I am in the Storm Zone, I usually feel worthless and unlovable.

☐ When I am in the Storm Zone, I often experience brain fog that makes it difficult to focus and concentrate.

☐ When I am in the Storm Zone, I tend to withdraw from other people because I feel too depressed to be able to engage with them.

☐ When I am in the Storm Zone, I sometimes feel numb – in the sense that I feel completely disconnected from the world around me, and unable to feel anything at all. When this is the case, then rather than "living," it seems as if I am merely "existing."

☐ When I am in the Storm Zone, I sometimes feel so irritable that I accidentally snap over something small or lash out at people when they do not deserve it.

☐ When I am in the Storm Zone, I sometimes feel so low that I cannot envision a happy future for myself, which destroys any motivation I have to do the things that I know are good for me.

☐ When I am in the Storm Zone, I feel so desperate to receive some temporary relief that I sometimes engage in self-sabotaging behaviors that I know are not good for me.

In particular, these self-sabotaging behaviors include (circle / underline / highlight the ones that apply): *"comfort eating"* / *substance abuse* / *overspending on "retail therapy"* / *self-harming*

Additionally, other self-sabotaging habits I sometimes engage in include the following:

☐ When I am in the Storm Zone, there are times when life no longer feels worth living.

Other symptoms I sometimes experience when I am in the Storm Zone include these:

_____
_____
_____
_____
_____
_____
_____

When I am in the Storm Zone and the intensity of my depressive symptoms are severe, some realistic / unrealistic expectations to have of me are as follows:

_____
_____
_____
_____
_____
_____

When I am in the Storm Zone, I would like to have people support me by doing the following:

_____
_____
_____
_____
_____
_____

Part 2: The Rain Zone of the Storm to Sun Framework

When someone is in the Rain Zone of the Storm to Sun Framework, it means that the severity of their depressive symptoms are moderate.

To identify what you tend to experience when you are in the Rain Zone, we once again encourage you to check the boxes that apply to you, and when prompted, fill in the blanks as well.

☐ When I am in the Rain Zone, although my negative thoughts are not as uncontrollable, intrusive, constant, or catastrophic as they are in the Storm Zone, I do still struggle with them.

☐ Although not to the same degree as when I am in the Storm Zone, when I am in the Rain Zone, I still experience difficult, painful emotions.

In particular, these difficult, painful emotions include (circle / underline / highlight the ones that apply): *sadness / misery / worthlessness / overwhelm / irritability / lack of motivation / shame / hopelessness*

Additionally, other difficult, painful emotions I sometimes experience in the Rain Zone include the following:

_____

_____

☐ When I am in the Rain Zone, my ability to function tends to be compromised.

☐ When I am in the Rain Zone, although I am able to fulfill the majority of my responsibilities, doing so leaves me feeling tired, run-down, and at the end of my tether.

☐ When I am in the Rain Zone, I usually feel too tired / overwhelmed to do all of the things that I would like to do that I know are good for me.

In particular, some tasks / activities that I often struggle to do in the Rain Zone include the following:

_____

_____

_____

_____

_____

☐ In the Rain Zone, it is sometimes beyond my capacity to be able to socialize with other people.

Other symptoms I sometimes experience when I am in the Rain Zone include the following:

_____

_____

_____

_____

_____

_____

_____

When I am in the Rain Zone and the severity of my depressive symptoms are moderate, some realistic / unrealistic expectations to have of me include the following:

_____

_____

_____

_____

_____

_____

When I am in the Rain Zone, I would like to have people support me by doing the following:

_____

_____

_____

_____

_____

_____

Part 3: The Cloud Zone of the Storm
to Sun Framework

When someone is in the Cloud Zone of the Storm to Sun Framework, it means that the severity of their depressive symptoms are mild (or perhaps even nonexistent). To identify what you tend to experience when you are in the Cloud Zone, check the boxes that apply to you, and when prompted, fill in the blanks as well.

☐ When I am in the Cloud Zone, although a negative thought might at times enter my head, it usually exits again pretty quickly.

☐ When I am in the Cloud Zone, I often feel positive emotions like hope, joy, and happiness.

☐ When I am in the Cloud Zone, it is possible for me to still experience difficult, painful emotions, but when I do, they are much more muted and fleeting than they are in the Rain or Storm Zone.

☐ When I am in the Cloud Zone, I feel pretty energetic, and do not feel as if my ability to function is compromised very much (or at all).

☐ When I am in the Cloud Zone, I enjoy engaging with other people and spending time with friends and family.

☐ When I am in the Cloud Zone, I enjoy doing my hobbies.

☐ When I am in the Cloud Zone, I do not feel as if I need any support for my depression.

When I am in the Cloud Zone, I like to engage with my friends and family by doing the following:

_____

_____

_____

_____

_____

_____

_____

Notes

Introduction

1. "Depressive Disorder (Depression)." World Health Organization, March 31, 2023. https://www.who.int/news-room/fact-sheets/detail/depression.

Chapter 1

1. Aaron Beck, *Cognitive Therapy for Depression* (Guilford Press, 1979).
2. "Depression (Major Depressive Disorder)," Mayo Clinic, October 14, 2022.
3. Ibid.
4. Deb Dana, *Anchored: How to Befriend Your Nervous System Using Polyvagal Theory* (Sounds True, 2021).
5. "Drugs and the Brain," National Institute on Drug Abuse, 2011. https://nida.nih.gov/publications/drugs-brains-behavior-science-addiction/drugs-brain.
6. "Depression (Major Depressive Disorder)," October 14, 2022.
7. Ibid.
8. Enisa Ramic, Subhija Prasko, Larisa Gavran, and Emina Spahic, "Assessment of the Antidepressant Side Effects Occurrence in Patients Treated in Primary Care," *Materia Socio-Medica* 32, no. 2 (2020): 131–134, doi:10.5455/msm.2020.32.131-134.
9. "Depression (Major Depressive Disorder)," October 14, 2022.

10. Nicholas A. Hubbard, Joanna L. Hutchison, Monroe Turner, Janelle Montroy, Ryan P. Bowles, and Bart Rypma, "Depressive Thoughts Limit Working Memory Capacity in Dysphoria," *Cognition & Emotion* 30, no. 2 (2016): 193–209, doi:10.1080/02699931.2014.991694.

11. "Depression (Major Depressive Disorder)," October 14, 2022.

12. Ibid.

13. Evren Erzen and Özkan Çikrikci, "The Effect of Loneliness on Depression: A Meta-Analysis," *International Journal of Social Psychiatry* 64, no. 5 (2018): 427–435, doi:10.1177/0020764018776349.

14. "Depression (Major Depressive Disorder)," October 14, 2022.

15. Enoch Ng, Caleb J. Browne, James N. Samsom, and Albert H. C. Wong, "Depression and Substance Use Comorbidity: What We Have Learned From Animal Studies," *The American Journal of Drug and Alcohol Abuse* 43, no. 4 (2017): 456–474, doi:10.1080/00952990.2016.1183020.

16. National Collaborating Centre for Mental Health (UK), *Self-Harm: Longer-Term Management* (British Psychological Society UK, 2012).

17. Erdem Pulcu, Roland Zahn, and Rebecca Elliott, "The Role of Self-Blaming Moral Emotions in Major Depression and Their Impact on Social-Economical Decision Making," *Frontiers in Psychology* 4, no. 310 (2017), doi:10.3389/fpsyg.2013.00310.

18. "Depression (Major Depressive Disorder)," October 14, 2022.

19. Ibid.

20. Ibid.

Chapter 2

1. David D. Burns, *The Feeling Good Handbook: The Groundbreaking Program with Powerful New Techniques and Step-by-Step Exercises to Overcome Depression, Conquer Anxiety, and Enjoy Greater Intimacy* (Plume, 1989).

Chapter 11

1. Sondes Bader, W. Abbes, M. Tfifha, M. Dhemaid, W. Mahdhaoui, and L. Ghanmi, "Warning Signs of Suicide Attempts and Risk of Suicidal Recurrence," *European Psychiatry* 6, Suppl 1 (2021): S589. doi:10.1192/j.eurpsy.2021.1571.

2. Christabel Owens, Gareth Own, Judith Belam, Keith Lloyd, Frances Rapport, Jenny Donovan, and Helen Lambert, "Recognising and Responding to Suicidal Crisis Within Family and Social Networks: Qualitative Study," *BMJ (Clinical Research Ed.)* 343, no. d5801 (2011): 343. doi:10.1136/bmj .d5801.

About
The Depression
Project

The Depression Project originally started as a Facebook page by Australian brothers Danny and Mathew Baker – Danny having suffered from depression from 2008 to 2012, and Mathew being a professional counselor. Both of them had a passion for understanding depression and mental health, so they began posting on Facebook in order to

- Help people with depression better understand what they are going through, and feel less isolated, alone, and misunderstood.
- Help people who have never experienced depression before to better understand the illness, and know how to support their loved ones through it.

Today, across Facebook and Instagram, The Depression Project has over three million followers, and their social media posts have been viewed over 10 billion times.

Books and Journals

In the course of running The Depression Project's Facebook and Instagram pages, Danny and Mathew had the opportunity to interact with countless people with depression, and read countless comments that The Depression Project's community members had left about the *obstacles that people with depression face in order to get better*. Most commonly, these included

- *"Therapy and counselling being too expensive"*
- *"Having to wait weeks and weeks to see a therapist – and then not even finding the session(s) very helpful."*
- *"Lack of motivation"*
- *"Lack of support and understanding from family and friends"*

Consequently, The Depression Project started teaming up with a range of different therapists and industry professionals to create affordable, accessible resources to help remove these obstacles. These include, among other resources

- Their books *Learning the Language of Depression, This Is How You Overcome Depression,* and *How to Support a Loved One with Depression.*
- Their *Negative Thoughts Journals* series, which help people with depression overcome the most common negative thoughts that The Depression Project's community members report experiencing – such as *"I'm a failure," "I'm a burden," "I'm useless," "I'm never going to overcome depression," "everybody hates me," "I can't do anything right,"* and *"I shouldn't be depressed because I've got a good life,"* for example.
- Their *Depression Journals* series, which help people with depression cope with and overcome extremely common – yet minimally talked about – aspects of depression, such as "depression lack-of-motivation," "depression numbness," "depression overwhelm," "nighttime depression," "morning depression," "depression anger," and "existential depression," for example.

- Their *Worrying Thoughts Journals* series, which help people with depression (and anxiety and other mental health issues) overcome the most common worrying thoughts that The Depression Project's community members report experiencing – such as *"What if they leave me?" "What if my mental illness only keeps getting worse?"* and *"What if my mental illness makes me unlovable and I end up alone?"*

Community Values

The Depression Project is deeply community-driven. They listen extremely closely to the problems that people in their community tell them they are facing – day after day after day after day – in order to understand the difficult, painful, complicated plight of people with depression as well as they possibly can. And, as they do so, they create resources to help solve these problems. It is for this reason that at The Depression Project, their slogan is *Creating a mentally healthy world, together.*

To learn more about The Depression Project and all of their work, please visit www.thedepressionproject.com.

Index